SENSORIMOTOR INTERVENTIONS

Using Movement to Improve Overall Body Function

Cara Koscinski, MOT, OTR/L

SENSORIMOTOR INTERVENTIONS

All marketing and publishing rights guaranteed to and reserved by:

(817) 277-0727
(817) 277-2270 (fax)
E-mail: info@sensoryworld.com
www.sensoryworld.com

Cover & interior design by John Yacio III

ISBN: 9781935567721

ACKNOWLEDGMENTS

I dedicate this work to Dr. Anna Jean Ayers, who pioneered sensory integration and tirelessly researched a set of complex symptoms now known as sensory integration. To Alex, for the brainstorming and your passion for creating sensory gyms and fun activities for kids. I extend my thanks to the members of the Sensory Integration Global Network, Dr. Lucy Jane Miller, and the STAR Center who care for their young clients enough to continue to research sensory integration disorders. I also dedicate this book to Carol Kranowitz, whose friendship I hold so dear. How I loved wandering the many rooms of the bookstore on our Oktoberfest excursion, realizing just how much our passion for books connects us. This work is inspired by those who struggle every day with Sensory Processing Disorder and the helplessness they and their caregivers feel, by those children who cannot speak for themselves yet feel the pain and frustration of Sensory Processing Disorders, and by those who see behavior as communication and find a way to give each of us a voice. I am deeply inspired by my own children who try so hard to succeed all day, every day, while living with the realities of sensory dysfunction. I express my thanks to those therapists far and wide who sent in photos of their precious students and clinics to enhance this book. I owe my gratitude to Jennifer Gilpin Yacio and Sensory World—a proud imprint of Future Horizons—who made this work possible and available to clinicians throughout the world. I also thank R. Wayne Gilpin, founder of Future Horizons, who believed in me and whose kindness I will remember always, and Rose, the editor of this book and new friend for her hard work and dedication. Finally, but most importantly, I extend my thanks to God who entrusted me with the amazing responsibility of raising children with special needs.

CONTENTS

FOREWORD

Think of Cara Koscinski as your "Pocket OT." If you care for a child with special needs, you might already be familiar with her previous pocketbooks. Her books offer reassurance whenever you need a quick refresher course, some positive support, or a practical, on-the-spot strategy. Cara understands the struggle of coping with a challenging child on a difficult day, and with her expertise tucked into your pocket or purse, she is right there with you!

Cara's reputation as an authority on children with autism, Sensory Processing Disorder (SPD), and other developmental differences is well deserved. She stands in a unique position as the mother of two sons with SPD, autism, and ADHD; as a therapist trained in sensory integration theory who practices occupational therapy using a sensory integration approach (OT-SI); as an accomplished author; and as a splendid communicator.

Cara has written for various audiences, and in this work, she writes for therapists who are knowledgeable about SPD and who seek to expand their repertoire of imaginative, fun, sensorimotor experiences for their young clients. Occupational therapists who have acquired the equipment and space as well as the art and science of providing intervention are best suited to implement the activities described herein. Of course, parents, caregivers, teachers, and other professionals are welcome to discuss these interventions with the child's therapist so they can adapt the activities for their own milieu.

This book is right up my alley. Like Cara, I care and write about our obligation to get ALL kids moving—not just the kids with special needs—in safe, appropriate, fun, and easy ways at home, at school, and on the playground. Although I'm just an OT-wannabe, unlike Cara and the therapists for whom Cara wrote this book, I applaud it nonetheless.

Sensorimotor Interventions explains in clear and concise terms how brain and body development occurs. If you are curious about brain development, you too may be fascinated to learn that babies' brains are chaotic until gazillions of sensorimotor experiences begin to organize them. You may marvel about how the masseter (an important facial muscle used for chewing) works with the whole body to hold up a person when his core strength is weak. You might have an "Aha!" moment when you learn how competing sensory information flowing into the vestibular system from the eye and the ear make it so hard for you to read in a moving car.

The "neuro stuff" Cara explains is fascinating, and the sensorimotor activities she includes are irresistible. For example, in the game "Get 'em Dirty!" the goal is to move muddy toys from one side of a bolster swing to the washing station on the other side of the swing. The real fun, to me, is the option to get the toys dirty instead of clean. Many a child would love the invitation to make a mess on purpose!

Obviously, I am a big fan of Cara and her work. We became acquainted in 2016 while presenting talks with Temple Grandin at a Future Horizons conference in Columbus, Ohio. We laughed about how frequently we must help people pronounce and spell our consonant-studded last names. We bonded when we discovered that "Baker" is her maiden name, my mother's maiden name, and my original middle name. We determined that Cara Baker Koscinski and Carol Baker Stock Kranowitz *must* be related!

Another much more important connection is that we both spend time thinking about the effects of SPD, autism, ADHD, and learning disabilities on children's development. All of us in our special-needs circle are better together when we employ fun, functional, physical strategies to help children, families, teachers, and professionals get in sync with each other. This book will take everyone who carries it in their pocket many steps closer to that common goal.

— **Carol Stock Kranowitz, MA**

Author, *The Goodenoughs Get in Sync* and *Preschool Sensory Scan for Educators (Preschool SENSE)*

Co-Author, *The In-Sync Activity Book*, *Answers to Questions Teachers Ask about Sensory Integration*, and *Absolutely No Dogs Allowed!*

INTRODUCTION

Like most expectant parents, I never considered there might be something different about my babies. I had no idea that the majority of my time during both of my sons' early years would be spent in speech, physical, and occupational therapy clinics. I couldn't imagine that various behavioral and developmental therapists would work in our home for many years with my children. As my sons' special needs became known, my hopes and dreams for them were quickly dashed, and our lives were thrown into absolute chaos; however, as the dust settled, we learned from some wonderful therapists who became like family.

As an OT, I continue to research and attend as many educational courses as I can to help my own children and those with whom I work. It's become my mission to learn WHY and HOW to provide help that lasts a lifetime. Through my work, I developed my course, Building a Better Brain, on which this book is based. You will learn that our bodies are biologically based on a pyramid. If we do not develop skills at the bottom of that pyramid, we do not form a stable base, and our systems may crumble when we least expect it. In fact, we see unstable pyramids in those children who are sitting at their desks, slouching over their papers and struggling to write even the simplest of sentences. We know children who continually seek sensory experiences by crashing and bumping into everything in their environment. Problems in behavior well beyond the "terrible twos" are seen in older children. In my previous books, *The Parent's Guide to Occupational Therapy for Autism & Special Needs* and *The Special Needs SCHOOL Survival Guide*, I encourage ALL caregivers and clinicians to read a child's behavior as his communication. This is critical to successful treatment and understanding. As therapists, we often forget that behavior is a form of communication, and it's become my personal mission to connect behavior perceived as difficult with a specific sensory or cognitive stressor.

The purpose of this book is to provide a step-by-step guide to therapists who understand the basics of sensory integration. Each clinic has its own set of different sensory equipment, and each provides useful benefits. In fact, vestibular and postural responses can be elicited without the use of any equipment; we will discuss that in this book as well. If your clinic does not have suspended equipment, we recommend that you contact a licensed contractor before adding equipment that bears a child/adult's weight. The viability of the support beams as well as their ability to support the weight of a client on a swing must be considered.

Contact the manufacturer of each piece of equipment to ensure that you are meeting all safety standards. Ultimately, your facility is responsible for carrying insurance should the equipment fail. The author of this book is not responsible for any injury related to any activity listed in the book. Furthermore, you should consult the maker of the equipment to learn guidelines for weight, installation, and clearance surrounding the use of the swing. Consult a medical doctor before beginning any/all treatment. Follow guidelines for equipment maintenance and complete regular inspection for wear and tear as well as defects. By purchasing, borrowing, and/or reading this book, you agree that you and your clinic are responsible and you release all liability from the author, Cara Koscinski.

Thank you for reading, and I'd love to see you at one of my Building a Better Brain courses.

Please contact me at ThePocketOT@gmail.com or visit www.PocketOT.com for additional information.

— **Cara Koscinski, MOT, OTR/L**

The Pocket Occupational Therapist

1. THE BEGINNING

Parents stare at their newborn baby with awe and wonder. What will her future be? Will she be good at sports? Will she be academically gifted? What will be her first word? How many children will she have?

The fact is that all infants are born with a chaotic brain. They are dependent on other humans to care for their basic needs and exist passively. Our brains are immature at birth and will grow and develop through various acts of nature, nurture, nutrition, and support (or lack thereof). Brain plasticity means that our brains will develop and change in response to the demands of the environment. Millions of nerves form connections depending on our genetics, environment, support from the community, and traumatic events. Our brain is quite remarkable, as it continues to evolve and change through wiring and re-wiring as we move through our daily lives. During these processes, called synaptic pruning, neurons that are no longer useful or functional to the brain die off, and connections that are used more frequently, continue to branch out and become stronger. The brain's complex network of connections looks much like a mature and healthy tree. The roots represent the nerves bringing information to the brain via the spinal cord (tree trunk), leading to the vast network of limbs and fruit of the tree's canopy. When a branch dies off, it's often pruned to give the other branches a better chance to develop and become fruitful.

> "Indeed, by 8 months of age, a baby may have an astounding 1,000 trillion synapses in his brain! This blooming of synapses happens at different times in different areas of the brain. Development then proceeds by keeping the synapses that are used and pruning away those that aren't. The pruning of synapses happens over the childhood years as the different areas of the brain develop" (Huttenlocher & Dabholkar, 1997).

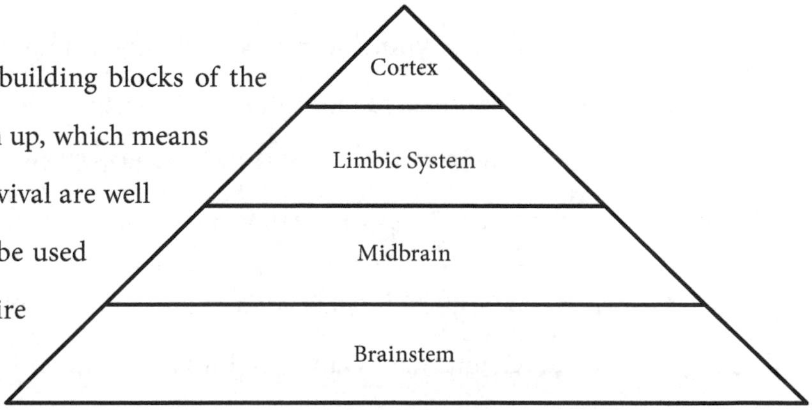

Scientists know that neurons are the basic building blocks of the brain. In fact, neurons form from the bottom up, which means that areas of the brain that are critical to survival are well developed, and those which will eventually be used for academic, emotional, and language require time and use in order to develop. Executive

Cortex
Limbic System
Midbrain
Brainstem

function skills do not mature until the mid-twenties! This process makes functional sense, as we are designed to possess those skills, which are critical to survival at each stage.

To illustrate, consider the breakdown of the developmental process when a baby is born prematurely. According to the Mayo Clinic, a premature infant commonly experiences respiratory distress, heart rate issues, and temperature and gastro-intestinal problems and is more likely to experience brain bleeds (http://www.mayoclinic.org/diseases-conditions/premature-birth/basics/complications/con-20020050). Babies' heart rates, breathing, and reflexes are designed to function for survival. If babies are not ready and have not had the time required to develop properly in the womb, the body is not ready to function properly at birth.

As a growing baby experiences life through her senses, synaptic connections form rapidly, and those that lead to success continue to become strengthened while those that result in failure are eliminated. This process is called plasticity. Like other neuronal growth processes, myelination begins in the primary motor and sensory areas (the brainstem and cortex) and gradually progresses to the higher-order regions that control thought, memories, and feelings. Also, like other neuronal growth processes, a child's experiences affect the rate and growth of myelination, which continues into young adulthood (Shonkoff & Phillips, 2000).

According to the Child Welfare Information Gateway,

> The development of synapses occurs at an astounding rate during a child's early years in response to that child's experiences. At its peak, the cerebral cortex of a healthy toddler may create 2 million synapses per second (Zero to Three, 2012). By the time children are 2 years old, their brains have approximately 100 trillion synapses, many more than they will ever need. Based on the child's experiences, some synapses are strengthened and remain intact, but many are gradually discarded. This process of synapse elimination—or pruning—is a normal part of development. By the time children reach adolescence, about half of their synapses have been discarded, leaving the number they will have for most of the rest of their lives. https://www.childwelfare.gov/pubPDFs/brain_development.pdf#page=2&view=How the brain develops

Often therapists receive referrals for handwriting, coordination, and behavior. It is our responsibility to recognize and understand the developmental pyramid and utilize a bottom-up approach to assessment and treatment. We tend to forget the critical developmental scaffolding that supports higher cognitive function. Additionally, there may be gaps in function or flimsy adaptations created that will potentially crumble as they struggle to hold up higher structures, leaving them precariously balanced and in danger of collapse.

2. *BIOLOGICAL SCIENCES—NEUROSCIENCE*

To fully understand the connections between our interventions and the neurology, we must delve into a bit of neuroscience. Remember that we are providing input that affects a child's brain, so we need to understand how this occurs.

First, consider the brainstem; it's about eight centimeters long, yet it provides many of the basic survival and reflexive functions of the body. It consists of both gray and white matter. It forms connections between the brain and body via the corticospinal tract (motor signals), as described below.

> Approximately 90% of the axons cross over to the contralateral side at the pyramidal decussation, forming the *lateral corticospinal tract.* These axons continue to course through the lateral funiculus of the spinal cord before synapsing either directly onto alpha motor neurons or onto interneurons in the ventral horn. The remaining 10% of the axons that do not cross at the caudal medulla constitute the *anterior corticospinal tract,* as they continue down the spinal cord in the anterior funiculus. When they reach the spinal segment at which they terminate, they cross over to the contralateral side through the anterior white commissure and innervate alpha motor neurons or interneurons in the anterior horn. Thus, both the lateral and anterior corticospinal tracts are crossed pathways; they cross the midline at different locations, however (Knierim, 2017).

The spinothalamic tract is ascending as it provides information about pain, temperature, and crude touch. Via the thalamus, this information moves to the primary sensory cortex. The homunculus (see photo on next page) is a diagram commonly utilized to illustrate sensations from various body parts. I encourage you to visit https://www.maxplanckflorida.org/fitzpatricklab/homunculus/science/ for a free download and interactive homunculus map. Knowing where your body is in space helps to plan and organize movements. According to a study by

Roley et al. (2014), published in AJOT, "children with ASD show relative strengths in visual praxis and deficits in somatopraxis; vestibular-related functions, including balance; and sensory reactivity."

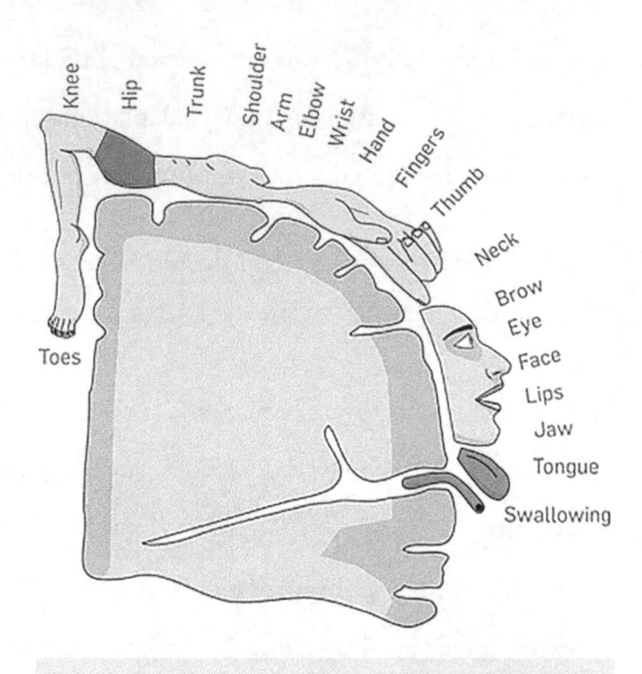

Homunculus sensory map used with permission from: Max Planck Florida Institute for Neuroscience; brainmapper.org

Proprioceptive, light touch, vibration, and pressure messages are modulated and move to the cerebrum via the ascending posterior column-medial lemniscus pathway. Furthermore, the reticular formation extends throughout the brainstem. It is the primary regulator of arousal and consciousness. The medulla oblongata contains neurons that connect the brain to the spinal cord (Dunn et al., 2016). The medulla oblongata is where 10 of 12 cranial nerves originate. Remember that vital survival reflexes such as swallowing, coughing, and gagging are integrated in the medulla. The pons is the bridge to the higher regions of the brain. Therefore, it's often called a relay station, especially between the cerebrum and cerebellum. In fact, in Latin, *pons* means bridge. Its function ranges greatly from facial expressions to regulating REM sleep.

Our midbrain is critical in the communication and control of the motor system, hearing, vision, and reflexes related to visual and auditory information. Remember that all of the neurons descending to the lower brainstem, cerebellum, and the spinal cord and those ascending to the diencephalon and cerebrum pass through the midbrain. Through various nuclei and smaller structures, vision (focusing, scanning, and blinking) is controlled. Additionally, the oculomotor nerve roots arise in the superior colliculi. Hearing and response to loud sounds (the Moro or startle reflex) are processed in the inferior colliculi.

Our limbic system is associated with emotion. It is a set of structures including the hippocampus, amygdala, and cingulate gyrus. When we move a memory from short to long term, we utilize our hippocampus. The Disney•Pixar movie *Inside Out* is based on a child's ability to form long-term memories. Our amygdala helps us by causing us to react to fear and aggression. It helps us when we are in danger but can be overactive in children who perceive sensory stimuli as a constant threat.

As clinicians, we understand that children often experience over-pruning or lack of formation of critical pathways within the brain, leading to dysfunction and missing skills that are critical to functional use. One of the possibilities is that the brain is not given the opportunity to experience an activity and thus form the pathway. This deprivation of experience then may lead to pruning or lack of formation of a critical pathway. One of the considerations of modern society include the use of "containers," which are designed to prop up or hold a baby well before he is developmentally ready to hold such positions against gravity all by himself. The infant's spine is forced into a certain position. Babies at this age are not physically equipped to shift and adjust weight. Additionally, the entire weight of the baby's head is placed on her spine, and the muscles and joints are not yet ready to support the weight against gravity. Physical and developmental complications may occur, including skeletal deformities, flat heads, motor delays, sensory deprivation, torticollis, and lack of reflex integration. Types of containers include car seats, nursing cushions, bounce seats, and infant swings. There's even a term for it: "container baby syndrome", denoting a baby who spends an excessive amount of time being propped up. Well-meaning parents purchase bright and colorful items designed to vibrate, bounce, and soothe baby. While not every baby spends too much time in containers, their frequent use and widespread availability tempts unsuspecting caregivers to purchase and utilize them more often than is recommended.

3. BABY'S SPINE VS. THE ADULT SPINE

The adult human spine forms an elongated "S" shape. Viewed laterally, these curves are the lordosis (two forward curves in the cervical and lumbar spine) and the kyphosis (the two backward curves in the thoracic and sacral spine). Their design naturally distributes weight, facilitates movement, and balances mechanical stress both at rest and during movement. They provide flexible support for the spinal cord through a complex bone, joint, and disc

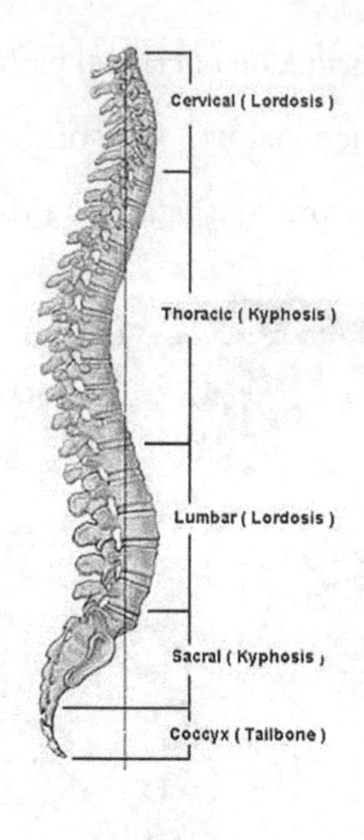

system. As we walk, run, and jump against gravity's pull, our bodies are well equipped to protect our delicate spinal cords and nerves, which innervate our trunks and extremities. Interestingly, an infant does not possess these curves. The spine develops the curves gradually as it adapts to gravity. As an infant grows in the womb, she is cramped in the flexed, fetal position. Her movements in the liquid-filled environment of amniotic fluid can be compared to beautiful acrobatics. At birth, infants exist in the state of flexion, still curled with spines in an elongated C-shaped (convex) curve, often called the primary curvature, as it remains in the thoracic spine. By design, this curve acts as a perfect springboard for her eventual gradual and purposeful movements against gravity. Additionally, it's the most efficient position for utilizing oxygen, feeding, and digesting (http://blog.intellidance.ca/blog/2-15-2011/c-s-how-nurture-your-babys-spine-development).

She first exhibits only reflexive extension via reflexes, such as Moro; however, she quickly springs back to her position of flexion. Through purposeful movement and via an intense and innate desire to explore her surroundings, she develops muscles in her neck to form the cervical spinal curve—the second curvature. This assists in balancing her head. As baby learns to sit, crawl, then walk, she develops the lumbar curve. In a typically developing baby, this process takes from 12 to 18 months or until baby walks independently against gravity, although the spine itself continues to grow until the teenage years. Therapists understand that, due to various developmental delays in social, physical, sensory, and cognitive development, not all babies can work independently through the process of developing spinal curves.

Working against gravity is critical for the prevention of skull deformities called flat head syndrome (plagiocephaly or brachycephaly). Infants often cry when lying in prone position, as this position requires them to work against gravity. Well-meaning caregivers (the author included) often become upset when baby cries and re-positions baby back into the container or into supine position. When my son was an infant, I often utilized a C-shaped cushion for my son. He quickly began to rely on the cushion in order to view my movements in the room. While I had no intention of causing any delay in my child, I unknowingly encouraged his dependence on the cushion instead of encouraging his tiny muscles to work against gravity. Also, work and play in prone position fosters visual-motor coordination, intrinsic hand strength, and separation by weight-bearing, and development of purposeful movements. Additionally, head shape becomes rounded as a result of lying or being propped up frequently in the same position. As therapists, we need to caution parents that an active, early approach to preventing those deformities and muscle problems caused by container baby syndrome is necessary to avoid lifelong consequences. This is especially true when infants are born prematurely or with special needs and physical deformities.

4. BRAIN DEVELOPMENT BASICS

The human brain has long been studied, and we are constantly increasing our understanding of its workings and processes. There are many functions, but the basics include the following:

1. Voluntary movement is driven by the brain and involves senses that we perceive and some that we do not perceive. For instance, our bodies sense our oxygen saturation, but we have no volitional control over the process. We do control our purposeful movement for functional tasks.

2. The brain performs perception of visual, hearing, smell, tactile, position, space, equilibrium, taste, and sensory information.

3. Homeostasis is the physiological skill set automatically set for survival. These skills include temperature, reflexes, ability to suck at birth, circadian rhythms, and many more, designed for the survival of our species.

4. Abstract functions or cognitive processes involving the emotions, learning, appreciation, and what makes us uniquely human. We have a conscious appreciation for our surroundings, are capable of love, and can communicate with language.

Via the processes of our brain and body, we are able to function in our environment; however, when a specific process is weak, others may take over. This is often the case when a person is blind and develops heightened senses in other areas. Our body can learn to compensate for weak areas.

- Connections are building into an organized state by 2–3 years of age.

- The concept of neuroplasticity explores how the brain changes in the course of a lifetime and how different areas of the brain can evolve and adapt over time.

Studies via functional Magnetic Resonance Imaging (fMRIs) have shown that, in utero, babies begin to develop connections between the visual cortex and eye movement in the third trimester (Medical University of Vienna. [2014, October 27]. Brain development in utero observed by researchers. ScienceDaily. Retrieved March 22, 2017 from: www.sciencedaily.com/releases/2014/10/141027085217.htm)

The following chart should be the most important visual used when therapists consider a child's function. At the very top, and when all else is in balance, academic learning occurs. It is often the job of the therapist to determine how to build up a child's motor and sensory systems so that he can succeed and perform to his potential. Remember that a child's occupation is to learn, and most times, this means spending his day at school. It's no wonder parents often come to therapy and report that their child "holds it together while in school but lets it all out when he gets home." Think of how much he's worked to help his body to focus on the task at hand, all while balancing the difficulties he may be having in basic body functions.

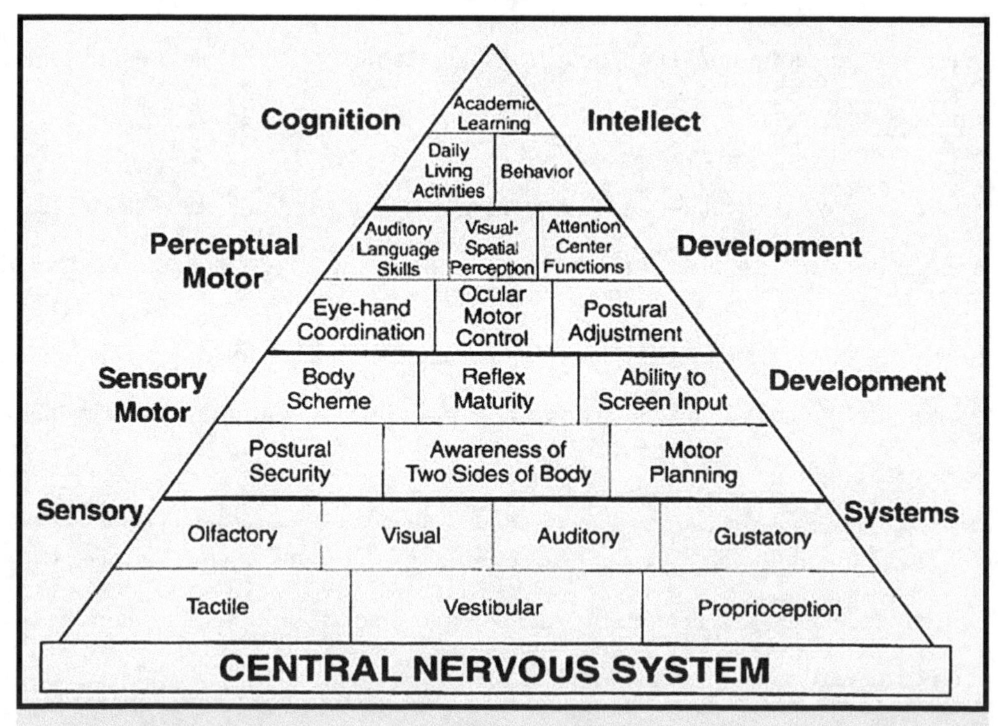

https://www.dealwithautism.com/forum/media/pyramid-of-learning-sensory-integration-disorder.80/full

This pyramid explains the components of Sensory Processing Disorder when it comes to learning and showing adaptive responses. The key components are:

- Cognition
- Perceptual motor
- Sensory motor
- Sensory functions
- Intellect
- Development
- Systems

The main subcomponents of sensory learning are:

- Academic learning
- Daily living activities
- Behavior
- Auditory language skills
- Visual spatial perception
- Attention center functions
- Hand-eye coordination
- Ocular motor controls
- Postural adjustments
- Body scheme
- Reflex maturity
- Ability to screen input
- Postural security
- Motor planning
- Awareness of both sides of the body
- Olfactory
- Visual
- Auditory
- Gustatory
- Tactile
- Vestibular
- Proprioception

5. CORE MUSCLES—A CRITICAL COMPONENT

As a new OT, I understood many concepts but it took years of continuing education courses in order to find my specialty area. This is the case with most new graduates; however, the most important thing is to keep learning. I lacked knowledge in the area of core muscles for at least 10 years of my career. I made improvements with my clients but could not take any of them to the next level of independence and overall strength. When my own children struggled to ride bicycles, hop on one foot, and complete demanding gross motor tasks, I fully realized that

in each occupational therapy assessment, a core muscle evaluation should have been completed. This is solely the base of the pyramid that provides stability for the top. In fact, we often see our students hunched over their desks as they struggle to write. I finally understood the implications of "W-sitting" (as pictured) after I studied and became competent in core muscle assessment and treatment.

Core muscles help in developing the body's midline. Our core muscles are critical for stabilizing, aligning, and moving the trunk of the body. These muscles help to protect the vital abdominal organs, assist with the Valsalva maneuver, help with energy transfer, generate movement of the body, and stabilize the top halves of our bodies over the bottom halves. The spine and ribs are designed

to protect the spinal cord and our internal organs, but consider the lack of bones between the rib cage and our pelvis! It's amazing to realize the core strength we need to support our bodies and even to assist in rotation in the transverse plane. When a student sits slouched over her desk while writing (or in a W-sit), her pelvis is in a posterior pelvic tilt, and this affects her ability to take in deep breaths and deliver critical oxygen to her brain. Thus, core muscles also help in stabilizing our pelvis. Movement against gravity causes a baby to help gain activation of the core muscles and refine them as they complete more purposeful movements. Developmental reflexes give way to function, and vision plays a key role in developing hand-eye coordination.

6. SIGNS OF WEAK CORE MUSCLES

Children with weak core muscles demonstrate many signs, which can be attributed to other things or are often overlooked. Toe walking is thought to be a sensory avoidance behavior that eventually leads to tight heel cords. In fact, my own son was seen by a physical therapist for serial casting after years of walking on his toes. One of the main issues the therapist pointed out to me was my son's severe core muscle weakness. In fact, after 12 sessions of therapy and casting, we learned an awesome home exercise program to help his core. He then began to play sports, and his handwriting and fine motor skills improved drastically! It's known that the masseter, one of our strongest muscles, lives in our face. It's designed to chew, but it is often used when children compensate for weak cores. In an attempt to find stability, they move their jaw into a stable position. Slouching over desks when completing fine motor tasks can be seen in every classroom. Children lean over and move their bodies as if swimming in their chairs in attempt to stabilize their bodies for distal coordination. Finally, rounded posture in shoulders, neck, and upper back is a common sighting in clinics. We use core muscle strengthening via the exercises listed in this book and kinesio-taping as treatment strategies.

NORMS FOR PRONE EXTENSION

Age	Median	1st Quartile	2nd Quartile	3rd Quartile	4th Quartile
4	43	0-1	3-17	18-42	42-82
5	51	0-9	10-30	31-60	61-130
6	48	0-48	53-62	63-77	101-241
7	49	13-61	62-85	90-119	120-186
8+	51	0-66	67-119	120-138	140-600
Learning Disabled	10	0	0-6	7-9	40-47

Norms based on research from Gregory-Flock and Yerxa.
Authors used the term "learning disabled"; please do not blame the author of this book.
There is an excellent assessment form located at the following link: http://www.therapybc.ca/eLibrary/docs/Resources/QUALITY%20OF%20MOVEMENT%20CHECKLIST%20FOR%20THE%20SCHOOL%20AGE%20CHILD.doc

Supine flexion norms for typically developing children were difficult to find. One study by Jeanne S. Sellers (1988) reported norms for children with special needs (See References).

The following study results by Marsha B. Lefkof were completed on 80 males and 80 females who were typically developing:

Subjects	Age	Scores in Seconds
Boys	3	15.5
	4	17.0
	5	27.4
	6	55.4
Girls	3	15.8
	4	20.8
	5	29.5
	6	52.0

7. VISION: CRITICAL COMPONENT

Our brain allocates a great deal of space for vision. This is critical in ongoing postural reflexes that maintain an upright posture. We recommend functional vision evaluations, as a child may become extremely frustrated if he is having double vision, sees words and letters float on the paper, and has headaches when reading, yet an eye doctor tells his parents his vision is normal. Remember, vision involves the brain as well as the eyes, so it makes sense that children with special needs might have dysfunctional visual systems.

As a certified Irlen Screener®, I'm quite familiar with the difficulties a child may have with vision. When visiting the Irlen.com website, try out different colors to see which best fits your viewing comfort. It is always shocking when children look at the visual distortion pages and say, "That's what I see when I read." The images are quite disorienting indeed, and it isn't until a child realizes that he's not seeing clearly that he can express his frustration with vision.

> The brain is like a system of roads. Information travels from one location to another. If the roads are direct and smooth, the travel is easy. If construction creates a barrier, the highway is blocked, and traffic is redirected into clogged side streets. There is still movement, but it is slow and frustrating. Children with severe visual dysfunction spend too much time on these side streets, and the simple act of perceiving the world becomes a nightmare. Children with behavioral problems typically have multiple sensory issues, and visual dysfunction is one of them. Eighty percent of the information we receive from our environment is visual!" (Fox, n.d.)

Remember that when an infant begins to crawl, she is working on her visual skills. An infant's visual skills will develop greatly as she realizes that her ball is either near or far from her location. This is called binocular vision and involves training the eyes to look off into the distance and then focusing back at the hands while crawling or reaching. We use binocular vision to calculate distances and make sense of what we see. It is a skill that helps us catch a ball, drive a car, and copy things from a blackboard. Spatial awareness is also built as babies crawl around and through various obstacles in their surroundings (See Figure 1).

8. THE SCIENCE OF VESTIBULAR SYSTEM

The vestibular sense is one of the first to develop and by five months in utero, it is fully developed. Movement of the mother's body stimulates the baby and provides a plethora of sensory information to the fetus (Jamon, 2014).

How does the vestibular system impact us? Its receptors monitor head position and movement and convey this information to the brainstem, where it is integrated into the motor systems. The vestibular system is important for maintaining equilibrium and upright posture and for control of synergistic eye movements. The combination of vestibular and proprioceptive input provides information about our position in space.

The force of gravity acts continuously on each of us. Information we receive tells us if we are moving, our speed of movement, and in which direction. Eye and head movement are coordinated by vestibular input so that we can respond to the objects around us. We quickly look at an object and determine whether it is moving or we are moving. Furthermore, visual scanning of our surroundings combined with our other senses gives us a perspective of the potential dangers and threats we encounter.

OLFACTORY	❖ System of smell ❖ Purpose is recognition & discovery ❖ One of most well-developed senses in newborn ❖ Assists in gastro-intestinal functions ❖ Elicits adaptive behaviors (breast feeding, rooting) ❖ Warns of potential dangers	❒ Week 5: Nasal pits present ❒ Nasal structure and components in place by Week 8	→ Sense of smell and taste are closely linked → Approach/withdrawal reactions present to olfactory stimuli → Recognition of mother through smell → Over-stimulation of system can lead to disinterest in feeding → Hypoxia can affect smell, which affects feeding interest
AUDITORY	❖ System of hearing ❖ Consists of external, middle, inner ear and auditory center in cortex ❖ Important for attention and learning ❖ Is motivating for alerting and orientation behaviors ❖ Basic to development of spoken language	❒ Week 4 – First anatomical division of inner ear ❒ Week 24 - System is structurally complete and functional	→ Preterm inability to habituate makes the auditory system very sensitive → Observed behaviors in response to increased auditory levels in NICU include: • Changes in color, heart rate and respiration rate • Desaturation in oxygen levels • Inability to sleep • Increased motor activity → Wait to introduce musical toys/tape recorders until after discharge (or greater than 39-40 weeks gestational age)
VISUAL	❖ System of sight ❖ Provides input for processing information to the brain ❖ Most complex system—one of earliest to begin development, but takes longest to complete ❖ Complements the vestibular system by correlating visual reference with equilibrium ❖ Strong connection between visual and tactile system ❖ Development continues from 40 weeks gestation to 3-4 months postnatally to increase differentiation skills	❒ Day 22 – Eye formation begins ❒ 2nd month – Retinal differentiation ❒ Weeks 6-8 – Optic nerve ❒ 3rd month – Precursors of rods and cones ❒ 22 weeks – All retinal layers present ❒ 23 weeks – Immature rods and cones ❒ 24 weeks – Myelinization of optic nerve begins ❒ 25-26 weeks – All neurons of visual cortex present ❒ 7th month – Eyes open ❒ 28-40 weeks – General rapid ocular growth ❒ 8th month – Iris sphincter develops ❒ 9th month – retinal vessels reach the periphery ❒ By 36 weeks – Awake visual alertness	→ Babies born earlier than 27-28 weeks gestation may still have their eyes sealed shut or cornea is hazy → No awake visual attention earlier than 30-32 weeks → Prior to 8th month, there is no way for preterm infant to control the amount of light into the retinal field → Behaviors observed in response to increased visual stimulation in NICU include squinting, shading face with hands, turning away → The visual cortex is one of the last to be myelinated, so higher levels of perception occur later (visual spatial relationship, visual motor coordination, visual memory, figure ground) → Long term developmental outcomes indicate visual perceptual deficits

The NICU Experience: Its Impact and Implications, Virginia Early Intervention Conference, Roanoke, VA; March 7-8, 2005.
Presenter: Barbara Purvis, M.Ed., NTAC Technical Assistance Specialist; *NTAC* (National Technical Assistance Consortium for Children and Young Adults with Deafblindness) is supported by the U.S. Department of Education, Office of Special Education Programs (OSEP). Opinions expressed herein are those of the author and do not necessarily represent the position of the U.S. Department of Education.

FIGURE 1 (CONTINUED)

Used with permission from Barbara Purvis

FIGURE 1

Prenatal Sensory Development

A sequential order of development and maturation is present in typically developing infants. This chart gives an overview of each sensory system, listed in the order in which the system matures to functionality and a brief description of the system's purpose and function. The last column in the table provides clinical observations and implications related to the sensory development of preterm infants, whose final weeks of development usually take place in the unnatural environment of an intensive care nursery.

Sensory System	Description	Maturation	Clinical Observations/Implications
TACTILE	❖ System of touch and reflexes ❖ Functions as a protection and discriminatory system ❖ Communicates sensory input from periphery to cortex ❖ Purpose is to establish identity and security within the environment ❖ Communicates both pleasant and painful stimuli	❒ Early fetal movement detected by ultrasound as early as 7 weeks ❒ Perioral area sensitive to stimulation by 7.5 weeks ❒ Sensory nerve endings in place and functioning by 11 weeks ❒ By 26 weeks primitive tactile reflexes can be elicited; rooting is present ❒ Back and legs modulate input by 32 weeks	➔ At any viable gestational age, infant perceives pressure, pain, temperature ➔ Entire system is extremely sensitive and easily over-stimulated ➔ Behaviors resulting from over-stimulation include pulling away from stimulus, squirming, crying, inability to settle/get comfortable, feeding aversions ➔ Perioral area is very sophisticated by 24 weeks ➔ Tactile defensiveness can be an over active protective response
VESTIBULAR	❖ System of balance and motion ❖ Function is to provide input from inner ear to vestibular center in brainstem ❖ Maintenance of equilibrium	❒ Day 44: Primitive semicircular canal ❒ Week 14: Sensory innervation completed ❒ Week 16: Myelinization completed ❒ System is functional by Week 21	➔ Impacts infant's state, ability to rest, ability to self-regulate ➔ Motion and position changes can be very over-stimulating ➔ Behaviors from over-stimulation include increased motor activity, color changes, crying, poor feeding
GUSTATORY	❖ System of taste ❖ Function is to transmit impulses to taste center in cerebral cortex ❖ Encourages exploration ❖ Facilitates developmental skills (hand-to-mouth, readiness for oral feeding, midline play)	❒ Week 4: Mouth begins to form tongue bud ❒ Week 8: Mouth and tongue development completed ❒ Week 20: Taste buds emerging ❒ Weeks 26-28: Withdrawal response to bitter taste ❒ Week 35: Differentiation between glucose and water with calming ❒ Newborn (Day 3 to 6): Differentiate between sweet, sour, bitter; between breast milk and formula	➔ Fetus sucks/swallows average of 1 liter amniotic fluid daily in utero; provides practice for feeding and self-regulation ➔ Preterm babies miss this practice or practice is confused because conditions outside the womb add new variables ➔ Infants have a high level of discriminatory taste; very easy to overstimulate this system ➔ Impacts infant ability in areas such as coordination of suck/swallow/breathe patterns and later feeding

Without a properly functioning vestibular system, we would not be able to maintain our muscle tone, and it is critical to effectively contract each muscle to complete a task. Isometrics, or holding our muscles steady, would be impossible without this system. Balance and equilibrium depend on the effective processing of information received throughout the body and especially in our inner ear. Depending on those signals, we receive messages that direct us to move in an effective way or respond to a demand such as minimize an unplanned fall or duck from a flying baseball. So, the vestibular system gives information to the body to help coordinate eyes with hands for visual tracking. Also remember that our bodies must work as a whole, coordinating both sides effectively in order to complete functional tasks, such as riding a bicycle and zipping our jacket. Any task which involves both our dominant and "helper" hand depends on effective vestibular function.

Activities to develop the vestibular system may include swinging, sliding, or using other equipment at the park. Do your best to avoid activities with excessive spinning or twirling, as movement in these planes can have negative effects including over-stimulation, lethargy, or changes in heart rate or breathing. It may also be challenging for your child to pace himself during these quick movement patterns. Encourage activities in which your child lies on his belly to participate in games or play with toys. Throughout your day, take note to see if your child seems better able to focus after completing a physical activity or partaking in activities that get him up and moving.

9. EAR ANATOMY AND PHYSIOLOGY

There's much more to our ears than many of us realize. The outer, visible ear is simply designed as a sound conductor. It's in the middle and inner ears where the magic happens.

There are five vestibular receptors in each ear; three are semicircular canals placed angularly. They sit in the horizontal, vertical, and diagonal planes and transduce rotational angular accelerations. Two otolith receptors, the utricle and saccule,

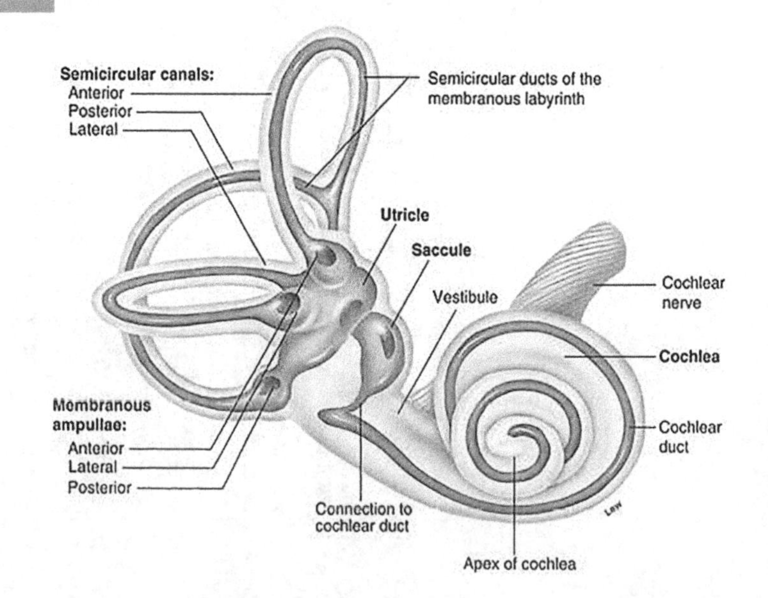

transduce linear accelerations. These gravity receptors utilize a layer of otoconia. This layer consists of a complex arrangement of minerals and organic substances that lies over the sensory receptor areas. A sharing force produced by the mass of stereocilia of the sensory hair cells allows for the detection of linear accelerations and gravity. "Disorders of hearing and balance are most commonly associated with damage to cochlear and vestibular hair cells or neurons" (McLean et al., 2016). "Eye gaze via vestibule-ocular tracts, vestibule-colic tracts innervate the neck muscles to support the head and vestibule-spinal tracts innervate the motor neurons of proximal and axial muscles of upper and lower extremities to maintain posture and balance. The vestibular system also has privileged relationships with the cerebellum through the vestibule-cerebellar and cerebello-vestibular pathways" (Jamon, 1979). Remember that many of us feel sleepy while riding in a car. This is because the constant horizontal (linear) motion creates a calming effect. Alternatively, when we utilize fast, irregular motion (starts and stops or frequent direction changes), our nervous system is stimulated, and as a result, our state of alertness increases. Why do we get motion sickness? Sometimes our visual system receives information that competes with our vestibular system. For example, I cannot read in the car, because my eyes see still words on a page, but my ears feel the linear movement of the vehicle.

Each of us has different thresholds for sensory input, and they can vary with each sensory system. So, while some of us may register low thresholds for spinning, we might be able to tolerate intense proprioceptive input. Consider an amusement park; there are rides designed for each of us: spinning rides, roller coasters, stop-and-start rides, antigravity rides, and the stationary park bench (which is where I prefer to be!).

10. PLANES OF MOVEMENT

One of the most important points of this book and my Building a Better Brain course involves the realization of and treatment planning for assessment of a child's ability to move in all planes. In geometry, we learn that a plane involves three points in space. This is important as we consider that our bodies move in a 3-D multidirectional manner. Remember from gross anatomy that our bodies are divided into planes of movement. The sagittal plane corresponds to dividing our bodies into right and left halves. The transverse plane divides our bodies with a horizontal plane at the waist, showing rotational movement and dividing us into superior and inferior halves. Our frontal plane moves longitudinally through our bodies, dividing it into anterior and posterior halves. Occupational therapists must remember that it is the functional deficit we treat, but we must find out why and where on the developmental pyramid a skill is lacking so that we can build a scaffold to support and develop it. Otherwise, we are only making temporary and/or short-term gains.

When assessing movement, it is imperative that therapists consider all planes. Many of us assess supine flexion and prone extension, which yields excellent information about body awareness/proprioceptive knowledge, motor planning, movement in the sagittal plane, core muscle strength, vestibular movement against gravity, and endurance. Have you heard the expression, "Kids walk like they chew"? While it seems rude or insensitive, my experience has shown me there is some truth to the statement. Let's use our knowledge of human chewing skills. In my earlier book, *The Parent's Guide to Occupational Therapy for Autism and Special Needs*, I spend some time discussing the powerful masseter muscle used in chewing. In fact, pound for pound, it's one of the strongest muscles in the body! So, its responsibility is to move the jaw up and down. Four muscles on either side of the head are responsible for mastication. Lateral pterygoid muscles depress the jaw and move it side to side (when working unilaterally) to work

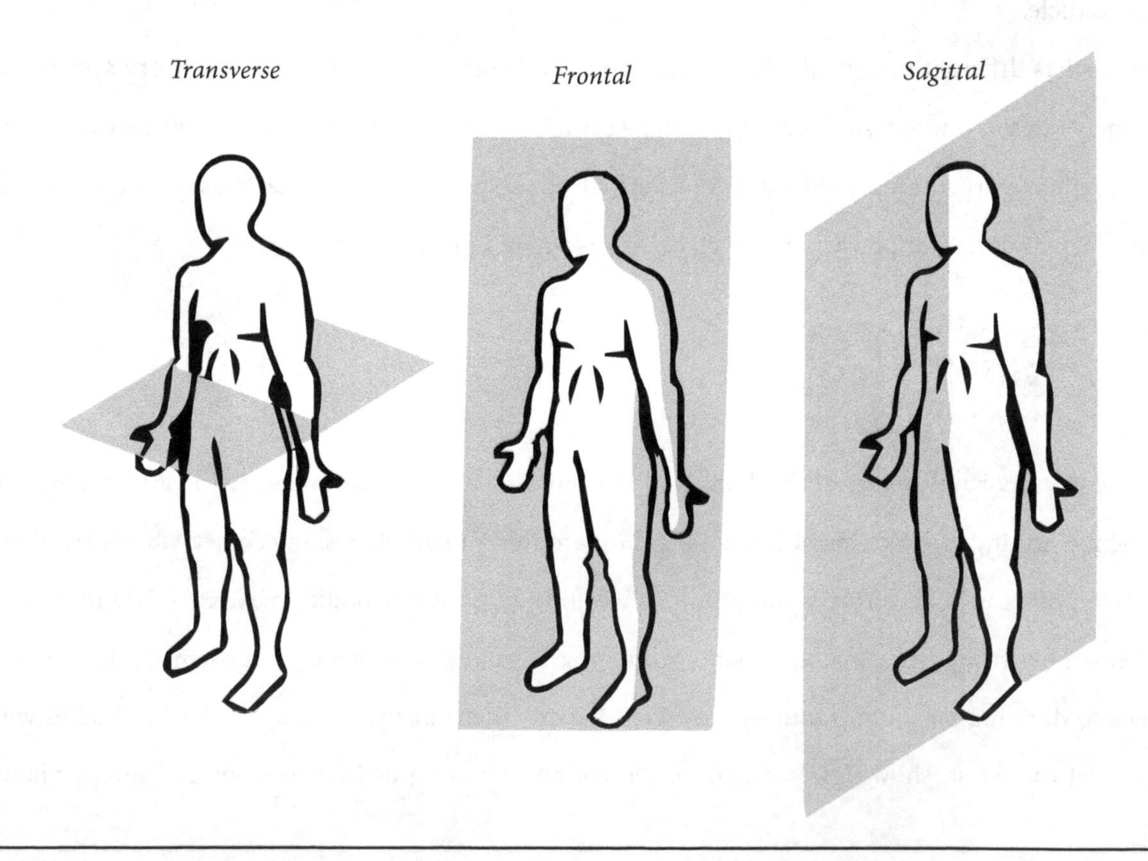

along with the tongue to move food (known as a bolus) for effective chewing. Medial pterygoid muscles elevate, protrude, and assist in side-to-side jaw movement. The temporalis and masseter elevate the mandible. So, with this combination, we are able to complete a rotary chew. Many children who seek therapy demonstrate immature chewing. This limits them to a vertical chewing pattern, which is inefficient since it lacks rotary movement.

11. AUDITORY SYSTEM'S CONTRIBUTION

The auditory and vestibular systems are intimately connected. Both of their receptors are located in the temporal bone of the skull. The vestibulocochlear nerve (cranial nerve VIII) branches off into the vestibular nerve and the cochlear nerve. Its function is to convey sensory impulses from the organs of hearing and balance in the inner ear to the brain. The vestibulocochlear system informs us of sound, movement, and orientation of space. The cochlear portion of the system turns sound or vibration into electrochemical messages that are relayed throughout the central nervous system and is critical to auditory processing. The vestibular portion serves to provide stabilization and influences attention and arousal, posture, and movement, thus serving a critical function in sensorimotor integration. The integration of our senses allows us to understand what we are experiencing in our world. So it makes sense that a program that would stimulate and help to integrate the cochlear and vestibular systems might be very helpful for anyone having sensory integration and learning difficulties. Receptors alert us to sounds and give us spatial information, which guides us where to look and on what to focus. By design, we startle with low frequency and gather direction/detail with high frequency sound. In fact, many therapy clinics incorporate rhythmic sounds into their sessions to organize and promote movement.

12. HISTORY AND GENERAL OVERVIEW OF SENSORY PROCESSING

Sensory processing has a complicated history and has evolved over time.

Sensory integration was first introduced formally at a lecture in 1963 by Anna Jean Ayres, PhD, OTR. Dr. Ayers was an occupational therapist (OT) and a developmental psychologist. While working at UCLA Brain Research Institute, she developed theories on SI. The terms *Sensory Processing Disorder* and *sensory integration* are sometimes used interchangeably; however, it's important to understand the origins of our understanding of the sensory system. According to the Autism Research Institute, "Sensory integration is an innate neurobiological process and refers to the integration and interpretation of sensory stimulation from the environment by the brain. In contrast, sensory integrative disorder is a disorder in which sensory input is not integrated or organized appropriately in the brain and may produce varying degrees of problems in development, information processing, and behavior" (Hatch-Rasmussen, n.d.). To better describe the difficulty so many have with processing sensory information, occupational therapists and many researchers use the term Sensory Processing Disorder, or SPD.

Humans are designed for survival. Through various sensory and motor systems, our bodies take in, process, and respond to the information around us. The sole purpose of the system is to determine what is SAFE for us. The sensory system works subconsciously and is out of our control. Designed to protect our bodies from danger, the sensory system relies on "pre-programmed" information and past experiences. As therapists, we know there are eight recognized sensory systems. Some of the most important are often overlooked by laymen, such as the vestibular, interoceptive, and proprioceptive systems, even though they provide information about the most basic survival.

The brain of an infant is akin to a garden, full of connections ready to be made. In order to be effective, some of the connections need to be pruned. The brain is equipped with micro ganglia whose job it is to prune and rake up the ineffective connections (Dr. Beth Stevens at Boston Children's Hospital, n.d.). As an infant experiences the world around her, she (either on purpose or by accident) elicits a change to her environment. She then realizes the change, and if it is effective or brings pleasure, it is repeated. Unknowingly, this forms new pathways in the brain, which lead to habits or behaviors that are listed as "successful." Efficient sensory processing makes the difference between living comfortably and experiencing difficulty integrating the various sensations, which bombard us throughout the day. *Proprioception* involves receptors in our joints, tendons, and muscles. The receptors provide information on body position, movement, and stretch. They monitor the position of joints and tendons and the state of muscular contraction. Tendon organs measure the strain on a tendon, and muscle spindles monitor the length of the skeletal muscle (Innvista.com, n.d.). Our therapeutic input lasts from two to four hours.

13. PROPRIOCEPTIVE INFORMATION

Occupational therapists work to develop concrete and evidence-based outcome measures for those with sensory processing difficulties (Schaaf et al., 2014). For those living with SPD, there is no question that life can be difficult. For both adults and children, SPD can negatively affect daily living. They avoid sensory-rich situations such as the fair, a museum, or an amusement park, thus limiting their pleasurable activities. Necessary life tasks, such as going to the bank, grocery shopping, or running other errands can be difficult. Adults will often alter the time when they run an errand, such as going grocery shopping very early in the morning when there are few people in the store. For some, driving can be difficult, since it requires paying attention to so much movement and noise at once. Those with SPD may have to narrow what they wear due to their sensitivity to clothing tags, tight waists, or seams in socks that can feel irritating or even painful (see Figure 2 on the next page).

Generally, a person with Sensory Processing Disorder seeks sensory input, avoids sensory input, and can seek or avoid different sensory areas. Every Sensory Processing Disorder is different, and the functional deficits vary greatly from person to person (see Figure 3 on the next page).

Sensory Modulation disorders consist of three types. Also included in the chart below are signs/symptoms of Sensory Discrimination Disorder (see Figure 4 on the next page).

Occupational therapists must thoroughly consider the complex patterns of Sensory Processing Disorder in order to fully "treat" their clients. Sensory-based motor disorders greatly impact an individual's functional levels. When posture and dyspraxia are not considered, treatment may fall short and desired goals may not be met OR may be based on splinter skills.

14. SIGNS OF A DYSREGULATED CHILD

- Is easily frustrated
- Worries and stresses easily
- Is impulsive, irrational, aggressive
- Is hyperaware of environment
- Has poor fine motor skills
- Has poor handwriting

FIGURE 2

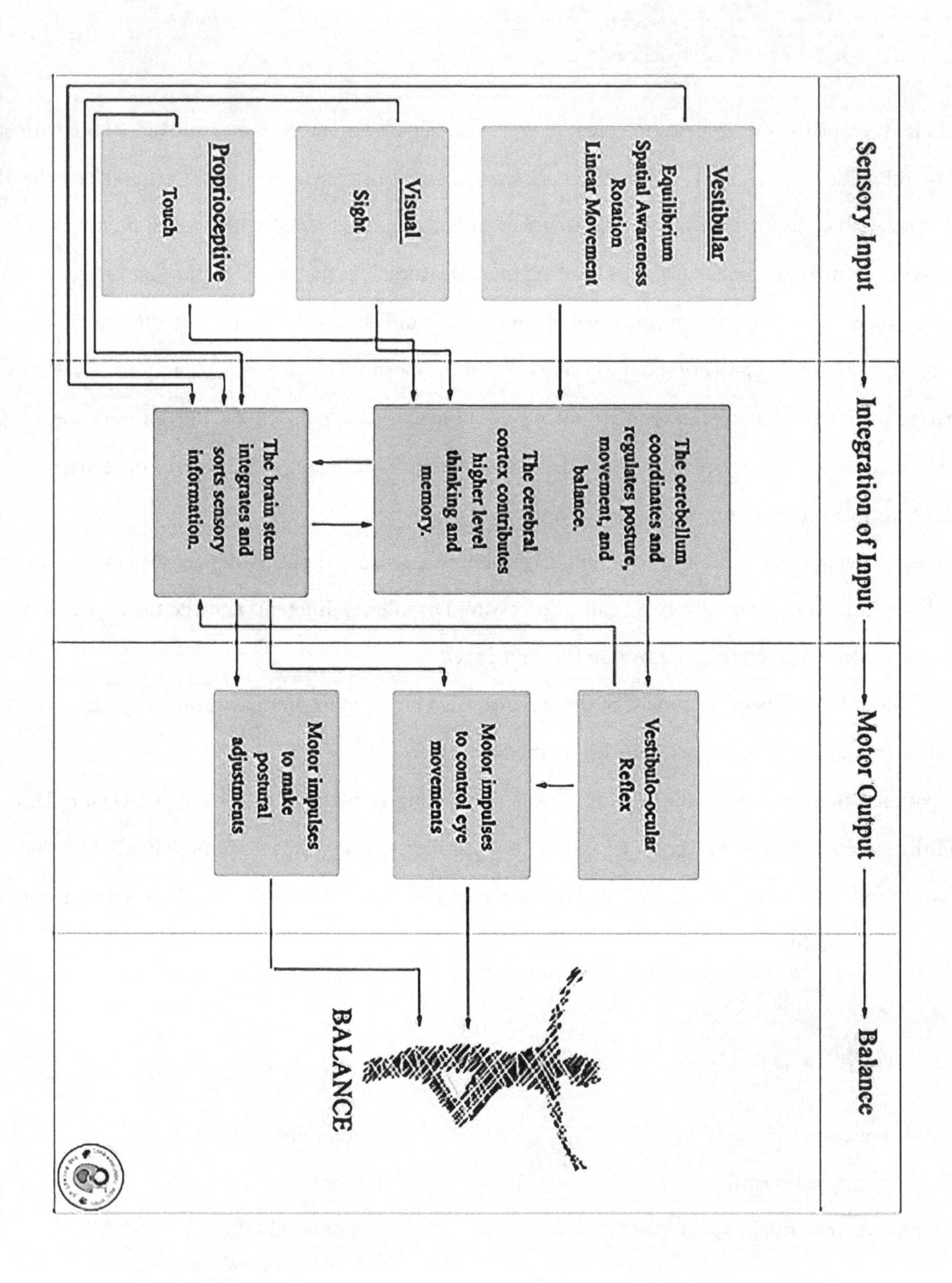
Sensory Input
Integration of Input
Motor Output
Balance
Vestibular
Equilibrium
Spatial Awareness
Rotation
Linear Movement
Visual
Sight
Proprioceptive
Touch
The cerebellum coordinates and regulates posture, movement, and balance.
The cerebral cortex contributes higher level thinking and memory.
The brain stem integrates and sorts sensory information.
Vestibulo-ocular Reflex
Motor impulses to control eye movements
Motor impulses to make postural adjustments
BALANCE

- Insists on routines
- Has difficulty with organization
- Experiences panic attacks
- Has difficulty sleeping
- Has difficulty toileting
- Demonstrates poor attention and focus
- Is distracted by or bothered by smell, sound, sights, and sensory information
- Experiences anxiety with unexpected touch
- Demonstrates physiological signs such as reddened/flushed face, sweating, increased heart and respiration rates, increased blood pressure, decreased oxygen saturation, shallow breathing, low energy, depression, sleeping difficulties, upset stomach, diarrhea, and constipation

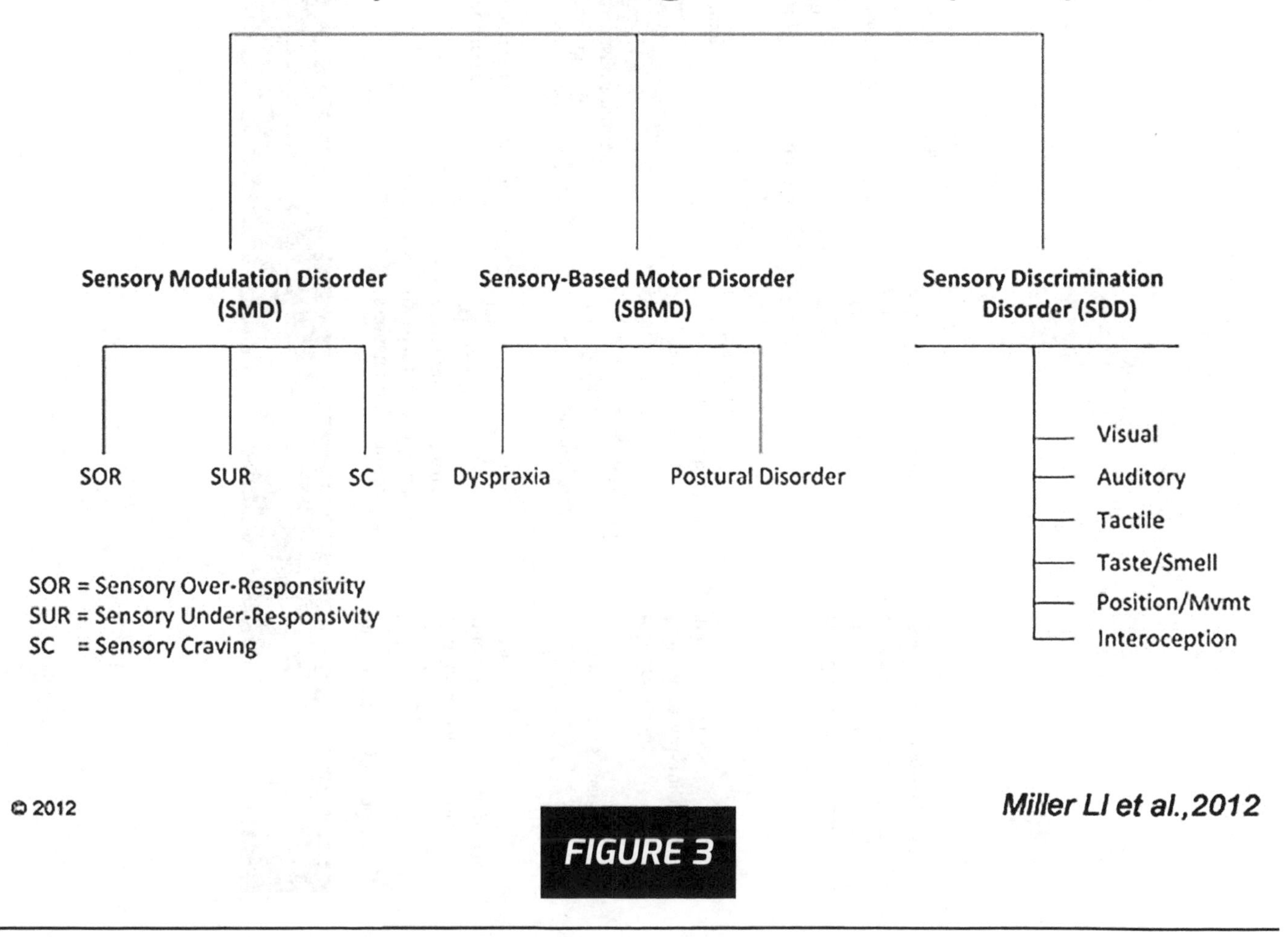

FIGURE 3

Type of Input	Modulation: Sensory Over Responsivity	Modulation: Sensory Under Responsivity	Modulation: Sensory Craving	Sensory Discrimination Disorder
Proprioceptive	– Avoids movement – Has low muscle tone – Fatigues easily – Struggles to develop hand dominance	– Falls onto floor – Craves touch – Kicks feet – Prefers heavy blankets – Grinds teeth – Pinches, chews, picks skin	– Is constantly in motion – Invades personal space – Often injures self when seeking out input – Plays contact sports	– Falls off of playground equipment – Seems clumsy – Cannot adjust/give correct amount of force to complete a task
Vestibular	– Does not use playground equipment – Avoids movement – Vomits/is often nauseous – Gets sick in car – Is fearful of uneven surfaces – Is gravitationally insecure	– Cannot sit still – Is in constant motion – Rocks – Seeks out movement – Craves running, spinning, jumping	– Loves being upside down and sideways – Cracks knuckles and stretches limbs – Does not get dizzy – Shows no signs of post-rotary nystagmus	– Demonstrates slouching posture – Falls frequently – Trips when walking on uneven surfaces
Visual	– Has frequent headaches – Squints in light – Must wear sunglasses/hat – Has watery eyes – Frequently rubs eyes	– Loses place in reading and math – Has difficulty tracking – Focuses on details vs. the big picture – Has difficulty with spatial relations – Reverses letters	– Stares at bright and spinning lights – Stares at moving objects	– Has difficulty with visual discrimination – Confuses/reverses letters – Has difficulty copying from the board

FIGURE 4 (CONTINUED)

Type of Input	Modulation: Sensory Over Responsivity	Modulation: Sensory Under Responsivity	Modulation: Sensory Craving	Sensory Discrimination Disorder
Auditory	– Covers ears – Avoids loud places – Makes noises – Is easily distracted by sound	– Acts deaf or does not respond to commands and/ or name called – Does not babble as an infant – Needs instructions repeated often	– Makes noises (often when it's inappropriate) – Plays loud music	– Difficulty adjusting voice to meet situation – Speaks with an accent or substitutes sounds
Interoception	– Does not eat enough, always feels full – Goes to the toilet often – Is sensitive to pain – Prefers sedentary activities	– Eats too much, even when peers are full – Constipated – Does not feel need to urinate until it's too late – Can become injured and not realize it – Prefers to remain active to keep heart rate high	– Enjoys feeling a full bladder and full bowels – Seeks out experiences that may be painful to others	– Difficulty telling the difference between nausea and hunger – Does not realize when she's had an accident – Is not aware of heart rate/ needs to take breaks to rest
Taste/Smell	– Eats limited number of foods – Vomits or is sensitive to taste/texture – Avoids strong smells	– Prefers hot, spicy, and strong flavors – Does not notice bad/foul odors – Stuffs mouth with food	– Smells others – Seeks odors that may be offensive – Stuffs mouth with food – Eats too much	– Does not mix food textures – Cannot tell if she is full or hungry – Consistently inconsistent
Tactile	– Avoids messy play – Washes hands frequently, often until they are raw – Prefers not to touch sticky items – Is sensitive to seams, tags, and/or a drop of water on clothing – Does not like clothing changes with season	– Seeks out messes – Feels things and people, even if it's inappropriate – Does not notice messy hands and face – Appears disheveled and messy	– Fidgets constantly – Drums fingers and bounces legs as if she cannot sit still – Seeks out experiences to touch items in surroundings – Cannot stop seeking touch and often is self-injurious	– Places non-food items into mouth – Seeks opportunities to touch things – Prefers certain textures but refuses others

FIGURE 4

Remember that children/adults who are constantly in a state of sympathetic stimulation are under control of hormones such as adrenaline and cortisol. They may be uncomfortable and need to regulate to a state of calm in order to relax and fully engage. It is our job to assist them through programs such as "How Does Your Engine Run?" and "Zones of Regulation."

15. DYSPRAXIA

Children with dyspraxia experience problems in planning, sequencing, and executing unfamiliar actions. They may appear awkward and poorly coordinated in motor skills. Many times, their inability to form motor plans causes difficulty with daily life skills, causing awkward grasp patterns on utensils and writing instruments. Because the formation of motor plans is difficult for them, they may prefer a routine and completing the same tasks often. In a study published in AJOT, Chu and Bodison (2016) stated that, "some children with dyspraxia have difficulties in force perception and joint position sense." The study utilized subscales of the Sensory Processing Measure and hand gestures. Knowing the signs and symptoms of dyspraxia assists in forming a thorough treatment plan. It is often reported that children with dyspraxia are often hypersensitive to noise, demonstrate head banging, are highly active, and often have feeding difficulties and/or allergies and sensitivities to various foods such as milk and wheat (Dyspraxiausa.org, n.d.).

16. POSTURAL-OCULAR DISORDER

It is well known that control of posture is a complex multisensorial task based on vestibular, visual, and somatosensory information, arising from sensory sources such as muscle, skin, and joints. Each sensory pathway has a specific activation threshold and sensitivity. Children with postural-ocular disorder demonstrate problems with control of posture and movements. They may demonstrate a difference in overall muscle tone and/or joint instability. Therapists note

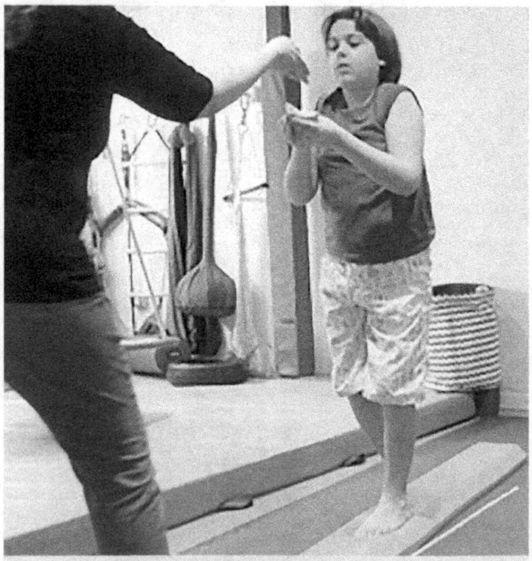

Joshua, a child with postural-ocular disorder. The Pocket Occupational Therapist clinic, Charleston, SC

that such children show slumped posture and flat feet and fatigue more easily compared to children of the same age (Merete et al., 2017).

17. SIGNS OF POSTURAL-OCULAR DISORDER

- Leans on desk and other furniture and slouches
- Chooses sedentary activities/avoids physical activity
- Demonstrates fine and gross motor skill deficits
- May have flat feet and low tone overall
- Seems weak and always fatigued
- Experiences anxiety with movement
- Seems to lose balance, is clumsy, or becomes injured more often than peers

Vestibular and proprioceptive problems as well as core muscle weakness are common. Functional vision, which involves scanning, tracking, eye-hand coordination, color vision, one eye being weaker or stronger, and shifting gaze, among other visual skills, is often weak. Functional vision assessments are recommended for children with special needs, especially those with eye-hand coordination deficits. Remember that visual cues help to stabilize the body, and when eye-tracking and other eye movement skills are weak, posture may be affected (Mallau et al., 2010). Since the vestibular system is responsible for letting us know our position in relation to our surroundings and gravity, our balance, postural muscles, and muscle tone are all affected when there's dysfunction. Additionally, there may be insufficient processing of both our vestibular and ocular systems in postural-ocular disorder. We need the two systems to work in harmony so we do not feel unstable and dizzy. Remember that the vestibular ocular reflex ensures that our visual field remains still when we move. I often feel as though our clients with postural-ocular disorder act/feel as though they are living in a "moving house." I cannot imagine how disorienting and uncomfortable it would feel if we felt as though our visual field and foundation moved each time we did! Mallau et al. (2010) wrote an excellent article on postural strategies: Postural Strategies and Sensory Integration: *No Turning Point Between Childhood and Adolescence.*

18. PROPRIOCEPTIVE SYSTEM FURTHER EXPLAINED

As humans, we possess the ability to sense our bodies' positions. In fact, we cannot adapt our motor control without proprioceptive information. So, when we desire to make a movement, our bodies must recognize the starting position of the limb as well as detect any force applied to the limb. We know that muscle spindles and Golgi tendon organs provide the necessary information. Furthermore, our reflexes must detect our position relative to our surroundings and spinal reflexes must maintain our balance in space. Via inhibition and excitation reflexes, we are able to spread the amount of work evenly across the entire muscle, so that all motor units work efficiently. That is, if some muscle fibers bear more of the load than others, their Golgi tendon organs will be more active, which tend to inhibit the contraction of those fibers. As a result, other muscle fibers that are less active will have to contract more to pick up the slack, thereby sharing the workload more efficiently. This occurs when we recruit additional motor fibers to assist when lifting a heavy load.

Our descending motor pathways modulate reflex circuits in the spinal cord. But remember that, depending on the circumstances around us, we are able to adapt the spinal reflexes. This is demonstrated as you lightly touch your foot into a perceived hot bathtub. Typically, you have learned not to plunge your foot into water which is thought to be hot, so you're able to modulate the withdrawal reflex! This illustrates how our reflexes are often combined with experiences to produce protective and functional movements.

19. INTEROCEPTION

Our eighth sense (and the subject of my new book) involves a sense that's been studied since the early 1900s. The awareness of the inside of your body, including heart rate and breathing, combined with or awareness of emotion defines interoceptive awareness. New research has revealed a definite link between interoceptive awareness and emotions as they relate to overall regulation, complex thinking, and sense of self. We know when we have to eat, drink, go to the restroom, cry, laugh, vomit, and take a deep breath, and we alone feel our own pain and joy. As with other sensory systems, a child may exhibit hyper and hypo-responsiveness in interoception.

20. AROUSAL AND REGULATION

Each of us must make sense of the countless amount of sensory information (stimuli) that flows into our brains each moment. Through each sensory pathway, information is detected and goes through our sensory system for handling. We need to determine which stimulus is important, which requires motor action, and even which reacts to the pull of gravity and the movements of our body in relation to our surroundings. The brain is responsible for organizing all of these sensations effectively for a person to function (including learning and behaving in an appropriate manner).

However, ineffective sensory processing can be extremely disorganized, and a true traffic jam or disruption may occur. In order for us to attend to our surroundings, we need to regulate ourselves. This includes adapting to the changing demands of our environment. None of us lives in a static world, and things change rapidly around us. Additionally, we need to form appropriate/adaptive responses to function effectively in daily life.

How do you regulate? When I'm stressed, I bounce my leg, chew on ice, and seek out a cold, fizzy drink. When I have room, I complete basic deep breathing and simple yoga movements. I WISH I could run around screaming and pounding my feet on the floor, but that would be socially inappropriate and even dangerous. Many of the children with whom we work do not have the maturity or desire to meet society's standards of appropriate behavior. Some cannot control their bodies since stress responses release chemical hormones that need time to be reabsorbed into the body. While this reabsorption is occurring, the goal is to keep the child safe until he is in a calm state. Self-regulation is complex and is society-driven to a degree. For example, one could run around and stomp in anger on a busy playground but not in a quiet library.

Self-regulation is necessary to adapt to the changing demands of the environment. Regulation is a physiological state. Since each of us has a different personality and temperament, we have different abilities to self-regulate and deal with the stressors and sensations of everyday life. Arousal refers to your alertness at any given moment. For example, lying on a beach chair listening to the waves crash causes a relaxed state. Standing at the top of a bridge, waiting to bungee jump stimulates adrenaline and heightened arousal levels. There are in-between states we move through as we progress through our day. Arousal levels dictate our attention and ability to form an appropriate response to what's going on around us. We quickly move to a heightened level of arousal when we must slam on the breaks to avoid a collision. We experience a rush of chemicals such as cortisol and adrenaline. We do not need those chemicals as we fall asleep and move to a state of calm and relaxation. The problem is that many of the children we work with have responses or regulation states, which do not match their surroundings. Furthermore, they may stay in a state of panic or low arousal that causes incongruence with their environment and is then disruptive to their ability to learn.

Emotional regulation is the ability to attain and maintain an emotional state that matches the task at hand. This depends on our setting, personality, and ability to regulate and balance our arousal. The fact is that we are only available to use certain moods at certain states of regulation. For example, when we are in a low-regulation state, we would not expect to suddenly jump up and down and laugh hysterically. As a result, our motor, behavioral, and mood depend on our state of regulation. Our sympathetic nervous system is known as the accelerator to our bodies. It is located in the thoracic spinal cord. When stimulated, it releases hormones, which cause us to fight, take flight or fright, and/or have a freeze reaction. Some children flee when in a panic situation, and this response may be quite dangerous, as they are not thinking rationally. Instead, they are driven solely by chemical stress reactions.

In contrast, the parasympathetic nervous system, located in the sacral cord, releases hormones that cause us to rest, recover, and digest. We consider this the decelerator to our nervous system. So, the sympathetic and parasympathetic nervous system engage in a constant interplay and our consciousness should match our environment/setting and what we are doing.

Here is a thought-provoking set of questions: Consider how stress affects our bodies and how trauma and fear of future trauma may keep our bodies in an elevated/heightened state of alertness. What are the long-term effects? What effects might childhood trauma cause during human development?

As children mature, they develop strategies that help them maintain attention and regulate their bodies. Children with Sensory Processing disorders often cannot regulate or form appropriate strategies. They cannot develop and/or refine their strategies as their surroundings change. Strategies such as using language for organization and planning, organizing of time to adapt tasks, making choices independently, and the execution and self-evaluation of strategies can be a challenge and lead to great frustration for all those involved. Additionally, difficulty regulating basic body rhythms such as sleep/wake cycles, hunger and thirst, hyperarousal, and low arousal manifest themselves in children who are not able to shift gears.

21. POSTURE IN STATES OF AROUSAL

In the beginning, infants exist in a state of flexion. They are either awake or sleeping, and their universe is quite limited. Think of the infant as a slinky. For the typical baby, flexion of the arms and legs is normal muscle tone, which provides a springboard for her movements. Additionally, the head and arms are kept at body midline. Now, consider babies born prematurely. They often lack the physiological flexed position and often look "loose and floppy." When lying on their backs, preemies must work harder to breathe. In fact, Kristin Grabowski writes, "positioning a preterm infant in a prone position, rather than supine, may prove to be a better choice. Premature infants are usually born with reduced muscle tone; therefore, positioning the infant on his or her side supports the development of flexor tone. Although swaddling has been used for years, adopting the method to be used for preterm infants promotes better organization, increased oxygenation, and reduced heart rate" (Grabowski, 2013). Maladaptive postures in infants contribute to decreased and even reverse spinal curvature; position in extension; developmental interference in the areas of motor, rotation, and disassociated movement; and flexor and extensor muscle imbalances. Additionally, problems with breathing, eating, and position of the diaphragm, and the tight upper trunk musculature may result from a lack of infants being placed in the flexed position.

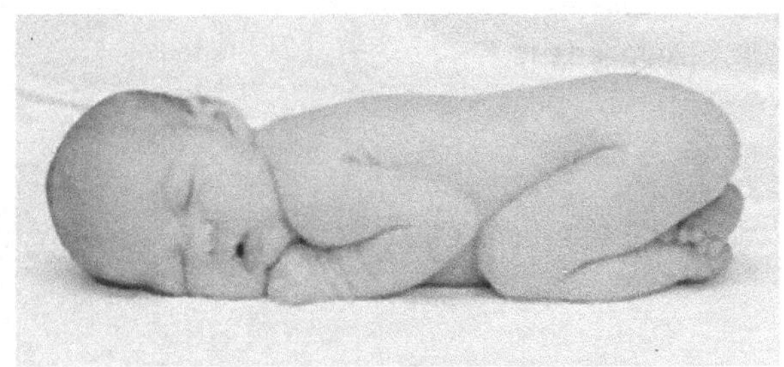

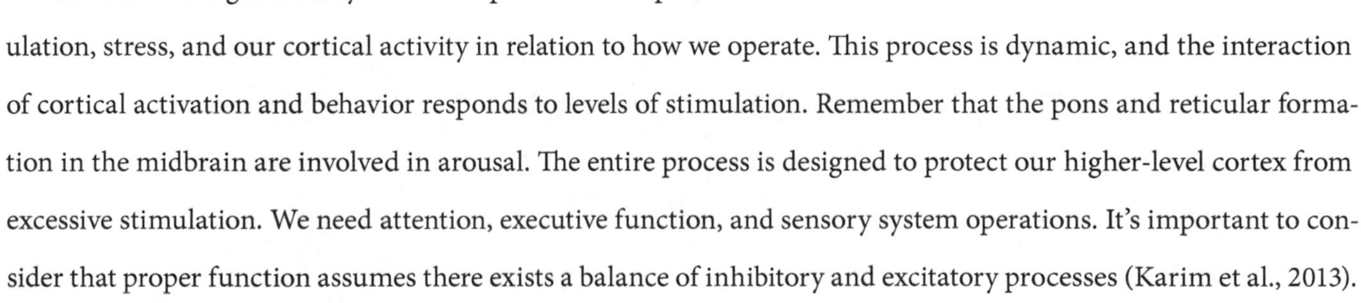

Arousal and regulation by definition provide descriptions of stimulation, stress, and our cortical activity in relation to how we operate. This process is dynamic, and the interaction of cortical activation and behavior responds to levels of stimulation. Remember that the pons and reticular formation in the midbrain are involved in arousal. The entire process is designed to protect our higher-level cortex from excessive stimulation. We need attention, executive function, and sensory system operations. It's important to consider that proper function assumes there exists a balance of inhibitory and excitatory processes (Karim et al., 2013).

The following are the levels of arousal and posture in relation to an individual's focus:

Level	Posture	Plane of Mobility	Attention	Behavior
Arousal	- Flexion & Extension	- Sagittal (flexion/ extension)	- On own needs	- Act on impulse/ reflexive behavior - Cannot or is just beginning to self-regulate
Alertness	- Lateral Flexion & Weight Shift	- Frontal (lateral flexion & weight shift)	- Task-based	- Beginning to act outside of own wants and needs
Awareness	- Trunk Rotation	- Transverse	- Responds to demands of environment appropriately	- Mature perspective - Asks HOW? - Can self-regulate according to demands of setting

(Ryosuke, et al., 2016; Chiba et al., 2013; Robledo, et al., 2012)

22. HOW DOES POSTURAL CONTROL DEVELOP?

Our bodies have built-in subconscious maintenance of body posture. As our movement and positions change throughout our day, postural reflexes help us maintain an upright posture. Gravity triggers our response, and as a result, these reflexes do not begin to develop until a baby is born. There are two groups of postural reflexes: righting reflexes and equilibrium reactions. Remember that our primitive reflexes were active until our purposeful movement occurred. Precious passive babies move from helpless balls of joy to living, moving, and active individuals who move freely throughout their environment. All but one of the postural reflexes arises from the midbrain. This means they are mediated from a higher center than our primitive reflexes. Therefore, their appearance means our nervous system is maturing.

Righting Reflexes	Equilibrium Reactions
Develop after birth and remain throughout life	Appear at 6 months and remain for life
Help with rapid loss of balance	Subconscious
Assist with integrated movements of head on the trunk	*Event specific
Order of appearance: • neck righting reflex • labyrinthine head righting reflex • oculo-headrighting reflex • body-righting reflex • segmental roiling reflex • landau reflex	Three types: 1. Moving the base: you move to maintain balance. Any movement you make to keep upright 2. Keeping the center of gravity over the base: you shift weight and/ or move arms, legs, and core to maintain balance within your base of support 3. Widening the base/lowering the center of gravity: think of a defensive wound—proactive extension, widening stance, parachute reflex (extension of arms in defensive response and why Colles or distal radius fractures are often seen with falls)

What are signs of immature postural reflexes? Therapists often see:

- poor body alignment
- difficulties with reading and writing
- sensory integration dysfunction
- gravitational insecurity
- anxiety disorders
- weak head control
- vision and gaze disorders
- bilateral integration difficulties

23. SUMMARY

Therapists often receive referrals for functional tasks which, on the surface, might appear random and inappropriate. In order to treat the whole child, as is the mission of occupational therapy, we must consider foundational areas when assessing and forming our treatment plans. In fact, we are often forced to work through behavior as communication, realizing that no one desires to fail. It is our great responsibility to be thorough and proactive in looking at all of the body's systems and making referrals as appropriate.

Consider yourself: Where do you fall? Does your mood match your setting? Are you able to regulate yourself through socially appropriate strategies? What if you did not care about following the rules of society? Treatment strategies must be meaningful to each person, as we are all a combination of our experiences and our genetics. We have the power to help improve a child's neurochemistry by choosing activities that increase dopamine and serotonin. As we seek to strengthen a child's muscles, body, breathing, confidence, and function, we are improving his or her future success. My favorite saying is, "We see the world not as it is, but as we are." I encourage you to have fun, be creative, and use this book as a springboard for your own success as a therapist.

24. POST-READING DISCUSSION QUESTIONS

- How does maturation of our sensory and motor systems improve school performance?
- How can you provide movement experiences to improve attention?
- What does today's classroom look like? How are children's bodies positioned at their desks?
- How do limited play, sensory experience, or floor-time opportunities contribute to decreased occupational performance?
- What factors in today's society are detrimental to building a strong foundation in both movement and sensory experiences?
- What plane of motion are you targeting?
- Which piece of suspended equipment can be utilized to target specific skill areas?

25. INDEX OF THERAPY SUPPLIES

1. Square or Rectangle Platform Swing
2. Net Swing
3. Bolster Swing
4. Bolster or Tire Swing on the Ground
5. Frog Swing
6. Balance Beam/Taped-Line Walk
7. Moon Swing
8. Standard Strap (Playground Swing)

Way to Grow OT
www.waytogrowaz.com

9. Trapeze and Monkey Bars
10. Barrel
11. YOGA
12. Crash Pad
13. Inflatable Dolphin
14. Scooter
15. Balance Board

26. RECTANGLE OR SQUARE PLATFORM SWING

Activity Theme #1

7-Position Moon Blaster Challenge (Space Theme)

SETUP: Hang the swing from two points of suspension. Place a moon swing on the 3rd linear hook.

DESCRIPTION: The child will propel the swing with rhythmic movement to bump the moon swing x20 reps/position then change to the next position while the swing is in motion.

Position 1. Prone

Position 2. Supine

Position 3. Supine with BLE only

Position 4. Quadruped

Position 5. Tall kneel

Position 6. Stand with staggered stance

Position 7. Stand with lateral weight shift

Southpaw Enterprises
www.southpaw.com

THERAPEUTIC BENEFITS: Improves bilateral coordination; rhythmic sequencing; trunk and core strength, stability, and control; vestibular and proprioceptive integration, planes of movement, praxis.

ADAPT/GRADE: Raise/lower expected goal, use wedges for trunk support, verbal/tactile/hand-under-hand cues to push-pull.

Activity Theme #2: Bucket Transfers (Tow Truck Theme)

SETUP: Hang the swing from two points of suspension and attach each of the two buckets with handles high up on swing's ropes.

DESCRIPTION: The child will transition from a kneel to stand and reach overhead to retrieve a toy car out of the bucket and then transition via a crawling position to the other end of the swing and rise to standing in order to place the car into the second overhead bucket.

THERAPEUTIC BENEFITS: Improves balance, joint stability, body-spatial awareness, motor planning, sequencing, sustained attention to task, transition through planes of movement.

ADAPT/GRADE: Hang the buckets lower, lower the swing, and stabilize the swing to prevent instability.

Activity Theme #3: Tent Hideout (Camping Theme)

SETUP: Hang the swing from two points of suspension with a tent covering (occlude visual stimuli) the swing.

DESCRIPTION: The child can lie down in the swing to focus on fine motor skills or relaxation with fidgets, weighted objects, whistles, and/or oral-motor toys.

THERAPEUTIC BENEFITS: Improves the decompress and decrease arousal state, relaxation, and increases focus due to decreasing visual distractibility, vestibular, and proprioceptive awareness.

ADAPT/GRADE: Open zipper to decrease feeling trapped or being afraid of the dark; leave swing flat on floor or raise only a few inches.

Chewigem USA, Oklahoma City, OK
www.chewigemusa.com

Activity Theme #4:
Theme: Monkey Business

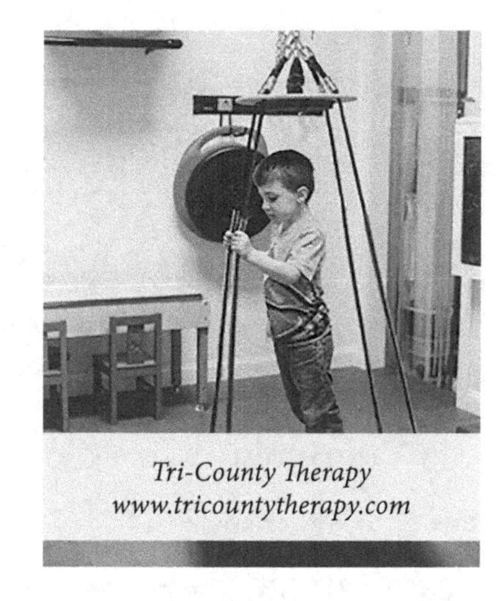

Tri-County Therapy
www.tricountytherapy.com

SETUP: Hang the swing from one point of suspension. Affix a barrel of monkeys, pipe cleaner with beads, or other stringing or connecting fine motor toy to the top of the swing.

DESCRIPTION: Children begin by standing on the swing and then slowly bend over to pick up a monkey to hang on to the affixed top area. Repeat.

THERAPEUTIC BENEFITS: Improves core muscle strength, vestibular and proprioceptive input, motor planning, fine motor, praxis, and movement through planes of motion.

ADAPT/GRADE: Begin with the swing suspended only inches from the ground OR suspended from two points. To grade up, move the swing gently while child completes the task.

27. NET SWING WITH OR WITHOUT PILLOW SUPPORT

Activity Theme #1
Search and Rescue Animals with Reacher (Zoo Keeper)

Maggie Peeler, MOTR/L

SETUP: Hang the swing from one rotational swivel point with stuffed, plastic, or printed animals spread out on the floor. Have a reacher readily available.

DESCRIPTION: Lying in prone position, the child will listen to the therapist sing an animal song and find the animal the therapist requests. The child will then use his reacher to retrieve the animal and drop it into a contrainer (aka a safari jeep).

THERAPEUTIC BENEFITS: Improves auditory processing, short-term memory recall, eye-hand coordination, visual scanning, vestibular and proprioceptive input, strengthening of extension.

ADAPT/GRADE: Therapist makes the animal sound, names the color, lists what it eats or where it lives vs. the name of animal (decoding); uses hand vs. reacher.

Activity Theme #2
Bridge Crossing (Logger)

SETUP: Hang the swing from one rotational swivel point with one crash pad on the right and one to the left of the swing. Place logs (aka long toys) on outside of the left of the crash pad and a box (aka fireplace) on the right side of the other crash pad.

Thérapie Kiddo Active Therapy, PC (Quebec, Canada)
Kiddoactive.com

DESCRIPTION: The child will reach for a log on the ground while kneeling or leaning from the crash pad and place it on the inside of his/her waistband or fanny pack, then transition into quadruped position to transfer onto the platform swing then off onto the other crash pad to place the log into the fireplace.

THERAPEUTIC BENEFITS: Improves core flexion activation and control, linear three-step sequencing, shoulder stability and hand-arch development, reciprocal coordination, and movement through all planes.

ADAPT/GRADE: Hang swing from two points for greater stabilization.

Activity Theme #3
Clothespin Clip from Vertical Rope onto Overhead Strap (House Keeper)

SETUP: Hang the swing from one rotational swivel with clothespins on each vertical rope and gather 10 pieces of small doll clothes.

DESCRIPTION: The child will grab one piece of clothing using the non-dominant hand then doff one clothespin with the dominant hand in a short kneel and then transition to standing on the swing to don the clothing with clothespin onto overhead strap.

THERAPEUTIC BENEFITS: Improves tripod strengthening, functional sequencing, bilateral coordination, vestibular and proprioceptive input, and core strengthening.

ADAPT/GRADE: Don clothing onto vertical rope with clothespin while standing, hang swing from two points if child has difficulty with balance.

28. BOLSTER SWING OR TIRE SWING

Activity Theme #1
Bolster Swing Transfers (Star Wars®)

SETUP: Hang two bolster swings (no more than 6' apart) parallel to each other, both hanging from two points of suspension.

DESCRIPTION: The child will straddle swing and pump with BLE to propel. Next, child will move legs and using back of knees as hooks, latch onto top of other bolster and pull himself up with BLE to transition to second bolster.

THERAPEUTIC BENEFITS: Improves motor planning, core muscle activation, balance, joint stability, vestibular and proprioceptive input, and movement through planes.

ADAPT/GRADE: Use rectangle glider swings vs. rectangle bolsters.

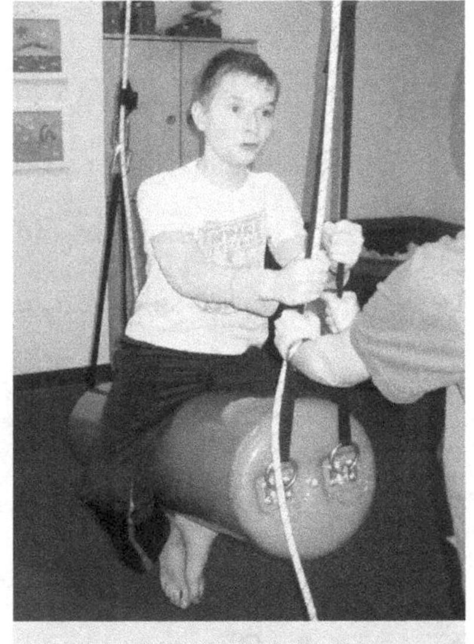

Susie Donohue, PT
Illinois

Activity Theme #2
The Hang (Monkey/Sloth)

SETUP: Hang the swing from two points of suspension with a crash pad within 5' away.

DESCRIPTION: The child will lay prone on top of bolster log and slowly rotate with flexion posture hugging with legs and arms around bolster until she is underneath, with full supine flexion underneath. The therapist will sing, "One for the money, two for the show, three to get ready, and four to go!" This gives the child the cue to release her body from the swing to move through space and land on the crash pad.

THERAPEUTIC BENEFITS: Improves core strengthening, timing in space, bilateral LE adduction, intense proprioceptive and vestibular input.

ADAPT/GRADE: Assist antigravity posture; child holds posture in side lying for decreased antigravity.

Activity Theme #3
Water Rescue (Lifeguard)

Tri-County Therapy
www.tricountytherapy.com

SETUP: Hang the swing from two points with tactile balls spread out on lateral sides of the child on the floor with a tire tube or large bucket set up at a 45-degree angle on the floor 8–15' in front of the swing.

DESCRIPTION: The child will straddle one end of the bolster swing with legs wrapped underneath. He will hold the vertical rope in front of him and use lateral trunk flexion to get to the opposite side to reach for a ball or beach-themed item on the floor, then pull back to vertical upright with bilateral hands on vertical rope, then throw the ball into the tire tube.

THERAPEUTIC BENEFITS: Improves core strengthening, vestibular input, proprioceptive input, midline crossing, and hand-eye coordination to accurately toss items into bucket.

ADAPT/GRADE: Do not hand swing, child completes activity on bolster or swing not suspended.

29. BOLSTER/BOLSTER SWING OR TIRE SWING ON GROUND

Activity Theme #1
Tippy the Canoe

Cara Koscinski, SC
www.PocketOT.com

SETUP: Place bolster or swing on the ground and have child straddle the apparatus.

DESCRIPTION: On one side of the bolster, place aquatic animals or anything related to camping, water, or beach play. Have child reach across her body's midline to pick up an item on the opposite side and move it. Pretend she's in a boat, and cannot tip, or else she will fall into the water! This is a great activity for puzzles, crafts, or any motor activity that fits the theme. Be creative.

THERAPEUTIC BENEFITS: Improves crossing midline, core stability and lateral trunk rotation, body awareness, and sequencing. Can add fine motor skills.

ADAPT/GRADE: Push child toward balls, and his work will simply be holding on with bilateral UE/LE.

Activity Theme #2
Get 'Em Dirty!

Tonya Cooley
www.TherapyFunZone.net

SETUP: Place bolster or bolster swing on the ground and ask child to straddle the apparatus.

DESCRIPTION: On one side of the bolster, place some mud and plastic animals, figurines, toys, or items of the child's interest. My clients frequently use Minecraft blocks and animals. The child must get the items from the dirty area and cross over to the bathing station and clean them up. This is awesome for any sensory play ranging from sticky and slimy to muddy and sandy. If desired, get the toys dirty instead of cleaning them up—this can be extra fun!

THERAPEUTIC BENEFITS: Improves crossing midline, core stability and lateral trunk rotation, body awareness, and sequencing. Can add fine motor skills and sensory play.

ADAPT/GRADE: Place the bucket or some of the items at midline.

30. ACROBAT SWING

Activity Theme #1
Cannon Ball Challenge (Pirate)

Limitless Performance and Therapy (Cedar Grove, NJ) Owner: Raina Koterba
www.limitlessnj.com

SETUP: Hang the swing up from four points of rectangle suspension with a vertical barrel on one lateral end and medicine balls on the other end.

DESCRIPTION: The child will be handed the lightest medicine ball from the therapist, then will crawl to the other end pushing or carrying it, throwing it over the edge into a vertical barrel, and then returning to the other side to retrieve the next heaviest ball.

THERAPEUTIC BENEFITS: Improves core stability and upper-body strengthening, body awareness, and sequencing.

ADAPT/GRADE: Therapist holds balls in front of child and gradually progresses so child crosses midline.

Activity Theme #2

Ball Bonking (Boat)

SETUP: Hang the swing from two points of wide linear suspension.

DESCRIPTION: The child will lie in supine with therapist holding a large therapy ball to bump the child's side with the child's choice of light, medium, or heavy force to propel the swing in rhythmic motion through proprioceptive input.

THERAPEUTIC BENEFITS: Improves rhythmic proprioception, decision making, and vestibular input.

ADAPT/GRADE: Sing a word from a children's song with each bonk (Chicka Chicka Boom Boom, ABCs, or Twinkle Twinkle).

Susie Donohue, PT
Illinois

Activity Theme #3

Obstacle Course Maze

SETUP: Hang the swing using four points (rectangle) suspension.

DESCRIPTION: The child will climb from the bottom layer to the second layer on the lateral side, then climb to the opposite lateral side to transfer up the third and fourth top layers. The patient will zigzag back down from the top layers, performing somersaults on the way down.

THERAPEUTIC BENEFITS: Improves vestibular-proprioceptive-tactile input, motor planning, neck/core flexibility and strength, and upper body and grip/pinch strength.

Southpaw Enterprises
www.southpaw.com

ADAPT/GRADE: Use a rope ladder to ascend up the layers; use the bottom of the Lycra for assistance.

Note: Southpaw's Acrobat Swing can be hung from two, three, or four attachment points. As a hammock, it provides vestibular input with increased pressure, offering a calming effect. The three- or four-point hookup increases the challenge by allowing clients to climb through the layers. It can also provide a calming tent-like space. This swing is great for developing body awareness and addressing motor planning skills.

31. FROG SWING

While in the Frog Swing, a client leaps and bounces on her hands and feet while supporting herself on her stomach in a lined sling. This method works exceptionally well with children who are gravitational insecure and have low tone.

Activity Theme #1: Old McDonald

SETUP: Hang the swing and play fun music or sing Old MacDonald Had a Farm.

DESCRIPTION: Lie in prone position in frog swing and place farm puzzle pieces around the floor. Call out an animal and ask the child to pick up the animal and toss it into a pretend farm 3–5 feet from the swing. This allows the child to have an area from which to pick up the animals one by one while rotating in order to toss animals into the farm.

THERAPEUTIC BENEFITS: Improves rhythmic proprioception, decision making, vestibular input, visual-motor coordination, extension strengthening, and core muscle movement and strengthening.

ADAPT/GRADE: Scatter puzzle pieces around the floor and ask the child to put the puzzle together (as seen in photo).

Jenny L. Clark, OTR/L, BCP and Abby H.
www.spdconnection.com

Activity Theme #2:
The Great Frog Adventure

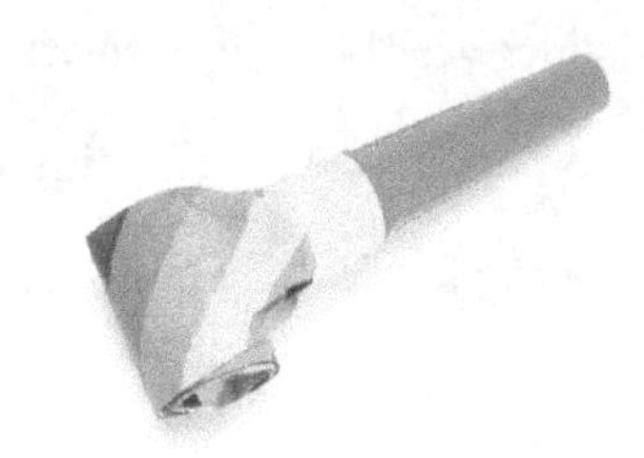

SETUP: Frog swing, bubbles, party horns/blower, container filled with bubbles and water with straws.

DESCRIPTION: Child lies in frog swing, but the seat is placed higher up so that both arms and legs touch the floor (child looks like a frog). Child takes hops to a rhythm sung to "Froggy Went A-Courtin'." She must only move to the beat to control her motion. After the song is finished, jump while blowing party horns to simulate a frog's tongue. Next, pretend to be a frog blowing bubbles through a straw into the water.

THERAPEUTIC BENEFITS: Improves rhythmic proprioception, praxis vestibular input, visual-motor coordination, core muscle movement and strengthening, LE strengthening, oral-motor heavy work, and self-control.

ADAPT/GRADE: Shorten activity or lower swing so that the child's feet touch the floor but she can still bounce up and down. Make more complicated by tossing/catching a ball to the rhythm of the song.

Activity Theme #3
Kangaroo vs. Sloth

Harkla
www.Harkla.co

SETUP: The child sits with her bum on frog swing. Play a CD of music that includes both songs with fast movement and songs with slow rhythmic beats.

DESCRIPTION: The child will use core muscles and LEs (holding on with arms) to bounce along with the rhythm of the fast beat. She can then relocate to the trapeze bar when the slow music is played to simulate a sloth hanging in the trees.

THERAPEUTIC BENEFITS: Improves core stability and upper body strengthening, body awareness, sequencing, LE strengthening, and self-control to transition from swing to swing.

ADAPT/GRADE: Toss/catch beanbags (imitating baby kangaroos and sloths) to the child as she sits in the swing to grade up. Use acrobat swing to simulate a kangaroo's pouch.

32. BALANCE BEAM OR TAPED LINE WALK

Activity Theme #1:
Circus Theme (circus performer, clown, ballerina, tightrope walker)

SETUP: Balance beam, pool noodles cut in half, or taped line with small textured balls randomly placed on both sides of the line.

DESCRIPTION: To begin, ask the child to walk heel to toe slowly, both forward and backward. Ask the child to focus on a fixed point on the wall. Next, ask the child to keep his feet on the balance beam while picking up balls placed on the floor. Ask him to toss the balls to you OR into a bucket either on the SAME or OPPOSITE side (depending on how difficult you'd like to make the activity and your goals). Play circus-themed music to add to the atmosphere.

THERAPEUTIC BENEFITS: Improves core muscle strength, balance, bilateral integration, hand-eye coordination, vestibular, and proprioceptive input.

ADAPT/GRADE: Ask the child to cross over his body midline by using his right hand to toss the ball into a bucket on the left side of the line. Use weighted or varied sized balls. Vary the thickness of the beam or taped line. Bounce a ball while walking on the taped line.

Activity Theme #2:
Simon Says (Balance Beam Square Dancing!)

SETUP: Provide a balance beam, pool noodles cut in half, or a taped line.

DESCRIPTION: Take turns with your student being the caller and the one who does the activities:

- Crawl on the line
- Jump on one or both feet
- Walk while imitating different animals
- Walk on toes
- Walk on heels
- Walk sideways
- Walk backwards
- Crawl
- Sidestep
- Move forward/backward
- Dance in different ways

THERAPEUTIC BENEFITS: Improves core muscle strengthening, proprioceptive and vestibular input, direction following, motor planning, and creativity.

ADAPT/GRADE: Change pace of walking; call out commands faster or slower.

Activity Theme #3
Rhythm and Beat

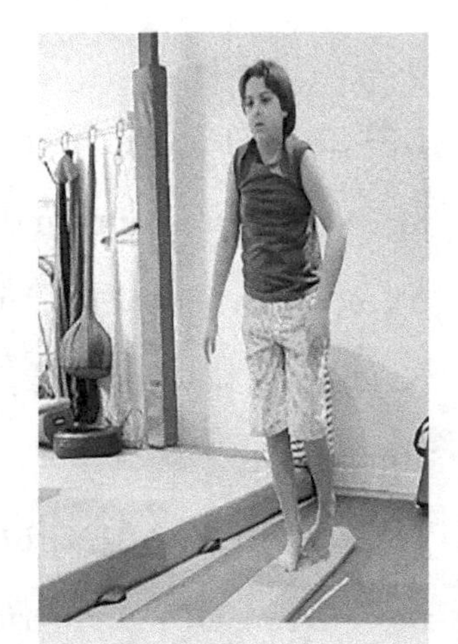

Bloom Children's Therapy
Charleston, SC
www.bloomchildrens therapy.com

SETUP: Provide a balance beam, pool noodles cut in half, or a taped line; metronome or music with a strong beat; and index cards with numbers from one to ten placed in both sides of the beam and within the child's reach.

DESCRIPTION: The goal is to move to a beat, so begin with the slow setting on the metronome or by clapping slowly. Ask the child to move on the beat and only on the beat. Ask the child to bend and pick up an index card and move to the beat according to the amount listed on the card. For example, forward three steps, backward six steps.

THERAPEUTIC BENEFITS: Improves core muscle strength, vestibular and proprioceptive input, motor planning, impulsivity control, and direction-following.

ADAPT/GRADE: Use only five numbers; therapist calls out numbers instead of child picking them up on her own..

33. MOON SWING

Activity Theme #1
Space Monkey

OT for Kids
www.ot4kidstlc.com

SETUP: Hang the swing and utilize a hanging rope, similar to a vine in the jungle.

DESCRIPTION: Play jungle-themed music and ask the child to hold onto the moon swing as tightly as possible while the OT pushes her gently. To encourage the child to maintain breath support and core, ask her to make different animal sounds, beginning with the monkey and other jungle animals. If she is able, reach to touch the "vine" (hanging rope), alternating hands.

Southpaw Enterprises www.southpaw.com

THERAPEUTIC BENEFITS: From Southpaw Enterprises' website: www.Southpaw.com:

> The Moon Swing is a great means for addressing bilateral coordination, balance, strength, and vestibular input. Its size and shape allow the therapist to create an easy mount and dismount for clients. The soft gooseneck is extra long to help the child hang on. The Moon Swing is exceptionally durable, with a ring connection point that is reinforced for extended wear. It comes with two inserts for different motor-planning possibilities. One insert is made of soft, fine bi-foam material that gives the client a swing with changing consistency and requires more difficult flexion patterns. The firmer insert allows the clients to stand, kneel, or complete complicated riding activities.

ADAPT/GRADE: Switch inserts for the swing, do not push swing—allow child to self-propel.

Activity Theme #2
Planet Challenge (Space Explorer)

SETUP: Hang the swing and gather large therapy and peanut balls. Place crash pad underneath swing (if swing can be placed high enough and depending on the child's height).

DESCRIPTION: The child will use his core muscles to propel and move toward each therapy ball, or "planet." He should try any means to move the planet off of the mat and out of his swinging reach. When he fatigues, crash onto the pad and pretend it's a planet that has a soft surface to be explored.

THERAPEUTIC BENEFITS: Improves core stability and upper body strengthening, body awareness, and sequencing.

ADAPT/GRADE: Push child toward the balls, and his work will simply be to hold on with bilateral UE/LE.

34. STANDARD (PLAYGROUND) STRAP SWING

Activity Theme #1
Blast Off (Rocket Ship)

SETUP: Hang swing from two points of suspension with a crash pad 2–6' in front of the swing.

DESCRIPTION: The child will pump with her trunk and BLE to propel the swing in a linear motion. She will count down from 10, then jump off at a high arc in space to land onto the crash pad safely.

THERAPEUTIC BENEFITS: Improves timing in space, core activation, bilateral coordination, and vestibular and proprioceptive input.

ADAPT/GRADE: Offer verbal cues to flex and extend legs, push off the tire tube with crash pad on inside on the floor to push off, and then land into with the swing low to the floor.

Activity Theme #2
Kick a Balloon (Outer Space)

SETUP: Hang the swing from two points of suspension with a balloon suspended from a string at the midline between two points that are 3–6' in front of the swing.

DESCRIPTION: The child will use his trunk and add BLE to pump to propel the swing in linear motion through space and use bilateral feet to simultaneously kick the balloon and repeat the sequence for a goal of 20–100 reps.

THERAPEUTIC BENEFITS: Improves bilateral coordination, fluidity of movement, and impulse control.

Activity Theme #3
Eye Chart (Cyclops)

SETUP: Hang the swing from two points of suspension with a vision chart or other reading material in front, hanging from a vertical surface.

DESCRIPTION: The child will pump in linear motion through space while reciting the letters, numbers, words, or symbols the therapist requests in a certain column and row on the chart.

THERAPEUTIC BENEFITS: Improves visual acuity, proprioceptive input, vestibular stimulation, and visual saccades.

35. TRAPEZE BAR AND MONKEY BARS

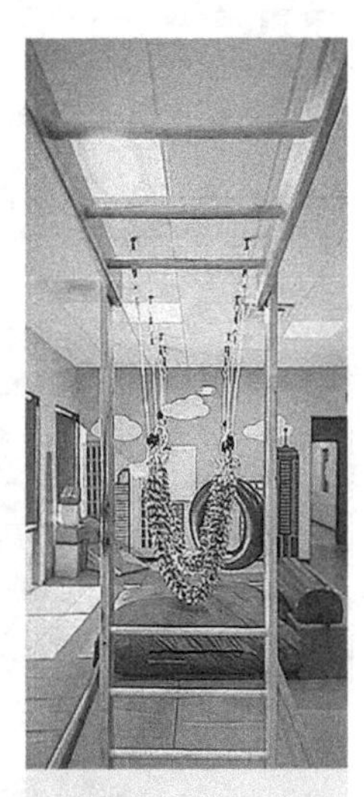

Way to Grow OT www.waytogrowaz.com

Trapeze and monkey bars offer many opportunities for children to explore all planes of motion. They'll have lots of fun with heavy work and motor planning, with the challenge to balance. If they prefer, they can grab onto the trapeze bar, and it's even adjustable to their height! Some trapeze swings come with a buoy ball swing, which supports your children with ADHD, autism, or Sensory Processing Disorder by encouraging strong motor planning, balance reactions, core stability, hand strengthening, and sensory integration.

Both activities promote flexion and extension, yet are flexible enough to allow for Skin the Cat and other rotation and antigravity movements.

Activity Theme #1
Can't Tag Me!

SETUP: Hang trapeze bar high enough so the child can lift both feet from the floor completely. Gather balls and beanbags of different sizes.

DESCRIPTION: Therapist tries to tag the child's feet by gently tossing balls and/or beanbags. The child must lift her feet up off of the ground in order to avoid being tagged. If she gets tagged, she must gather all of the beanbags while lying prone on a scooter board and return them to the therapist.

THERAPEUTIC BENEFITS: Improves core stability and upper-body strengthening, body awareness, sequencing, and movement in planes.

ADAPT/GRADE: Lower swing to grade down. To grade up, raise trapeze bar and/or increase speed while tossing beanbags.

Activity Theme #2
Astronaut Excursion

SETUP: Hang the swing and gather large therapy and peanut balls. Place crash pad underneath the swing (if the swing can be placed high enough and depending on child's height).

DESCRIPTION: The child will use his core muscles to propel and move toward each therapy ball or "planet." He should try any means to move the planet off of the mat and out of his swing reach. When he fatigues, he can crash onto the pad and pretend it's a planet that has a soft surface to be explored.

THERAPEUTIC BENEFITS: Improves core stability and upper body strengthening, body awareness, and sequencing.

ADAPT/GRADE: Push child toward balls, and his work will simply be to hold on with bilateral UE/LE.

36. BARREL

Activity Themes

Southpaw Enterprises
www.southpaw.com

The barrel is a versatile piece of equipment that can be used alone or with any other activity. Here are some of my favorite ideas for barrel fun:

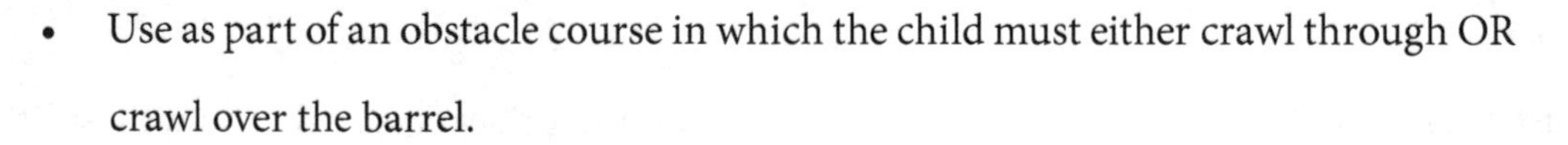

- Use as part of an obstacle course in which the child must either crawl through OR crawl over the barrel.
- Ask the child to lie in prone position over the barrel and support herself as she leans forward to pick up beanbags and tosses them into a bin, complete puzzles, and even blow bubbles or other oral-motor tasks.
- The child can sit atop the barrel and complete midline crossing activities. The feet can be supported by beanbags, foam blocks, crash pad, and other items found in the gym.
- Lying in supine position, the barrel provides a great stretch to the back as you support the child in a comfortable extended position. Always use a mat and a crash pad near the head to protect it. This is a difficult position for children who are gravitationally insecure and should be reserved to develop more advanced skills. Additionally, ask the child to extend her arms to protect herself and reach for the floor.

37. YOGA

Yoga is one of the best activities for strengthening core, breathing, proprioceptive, vestibular, crossing midline, and motor planning. When in school districts, remember that yoga does not have to be spiritual, rather a discipline of caring for yourself and respecting the environment and those around you.

One of the basic principles of yoga is that you should flex and then extend. Move to one side and then to the other. Balance is important, and the same is true as we teach our clients that they should keep balance and maintain regulation to support their body's health.

Breathing properly is critical in yoga and can help children learn how to take deep breaths that bring wonderful oxygen to their brains. Remember that our diaphragms are a muscular membrane, which separates our lungs from our abdominal cavities. When taking deep breaths, focus on bringing air all the way down to the lower abdomen. Children can place their hands on their navels for a cue. Sometimes children need to open their mouths while exhaling, making a HAAAAHHHHHH sound. One of the most important things to teach children is NOT to hold their breath, and when things get hard, they should remember to BREATHE!

Jenny L. Clark, OTR/L, BCP and Abby H. www.spdconnection.com

1. Child's pose is one of the most relaxing positions and provides an excellent stretch for those who have low tone or slouch regularly.

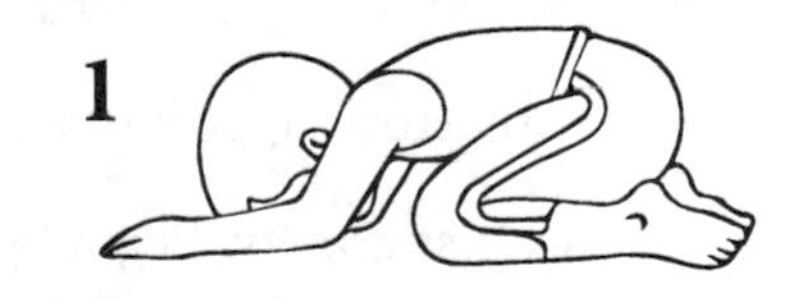

2. By reaching over their heads and leaning side to side, children stretch the core and work on lateral trunk flexion.

3. Kneeling and working on the same arms over head stretches improve balance as well as core muscle stabilization. Make sure to work on both the left and right sides to maintain balance.

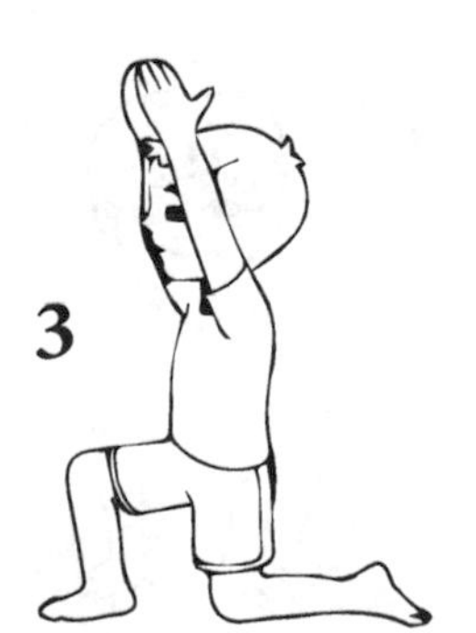

4. Cat position arches the back, and cow is when the child looks up toward the sky to lower the back and pelvis (opposite of cat).

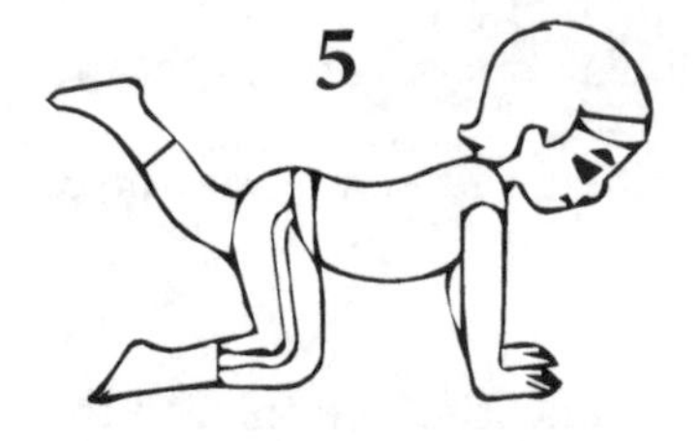

5. To add difficulty to the positions, raise the leg up.

6. Cobra pose is wonderful for working on UE strengthening and body extension.

7. Warrior (or hare to stick with the animal theme) is a STRONG pose. Children often repeat a mantra or positive phrase about themselves to boost their self-esteem when in warrior pose. It's wonderful for core, UE/LE strengthening, proprioceptive and vestibular input.

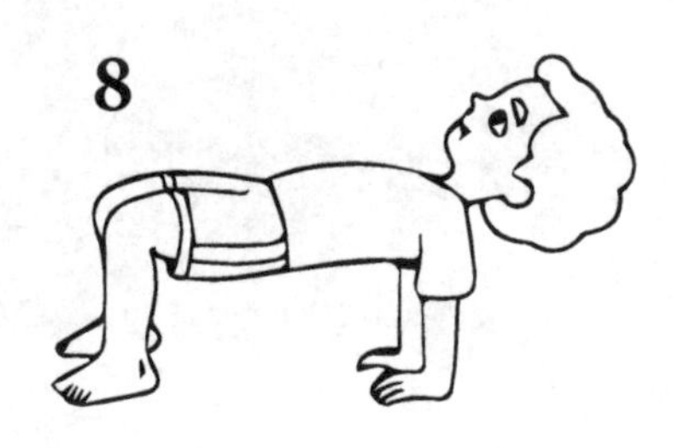

8. Table pose is a challenge for children who do not know where their bodies are in space. Most will need support to the mid-back area when beginning this pose. We often add this into obstacle courses as a human bridge.

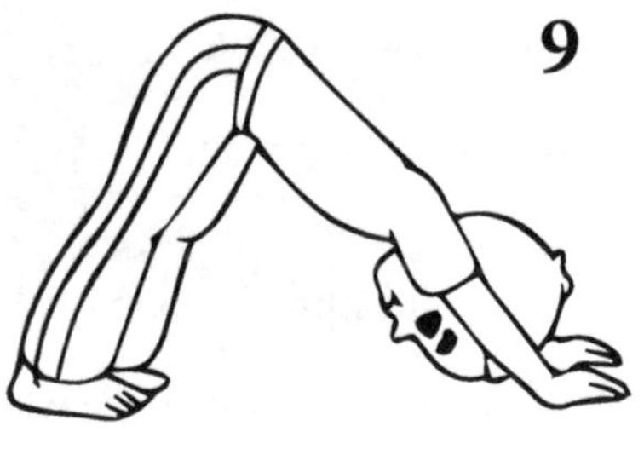

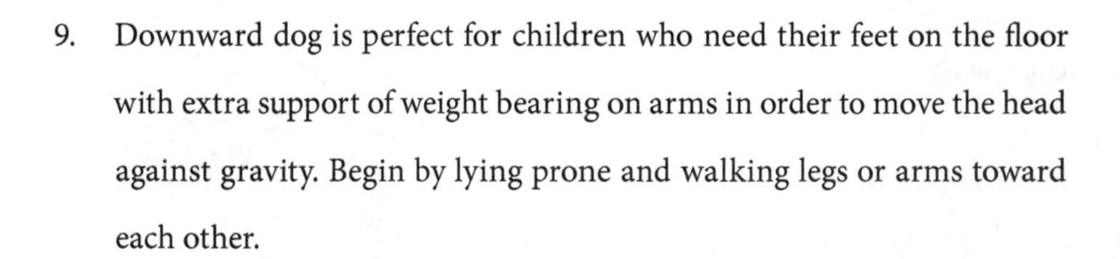

9. Downward dog is perfect for children who need their feet on the floor with extra support of weight bearing on arms in order to move the head against gravity. Begin by lying prone and walking legs or arms toward each other.

10. Froggie position truly gives proprioceptive input while keeping the head upright. It's a great position to stretch the legs. Adding this to the Frog Swing activity could really be fun and boost pretend play skills!

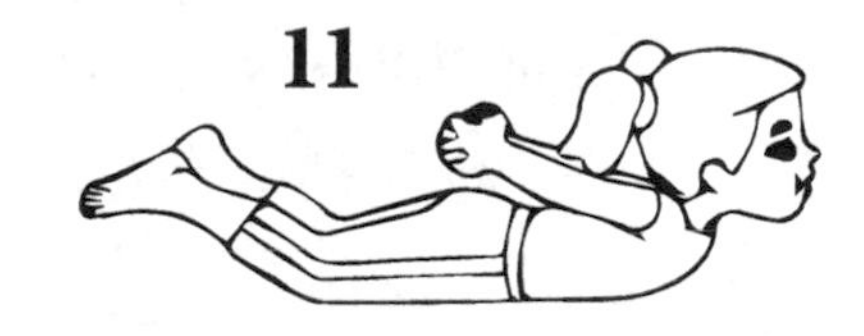

11. Shark is what therapists like to call prone extension. It's one of the best positions for assessing a child's ability to work against gravity. Grade up the activity by clasping the hands together to make the "fin" behind the back. Assess not only how long a child can stay in this position but also how he or she gets into the position. Are the child's movements rough and jerky or smooth and fluid?

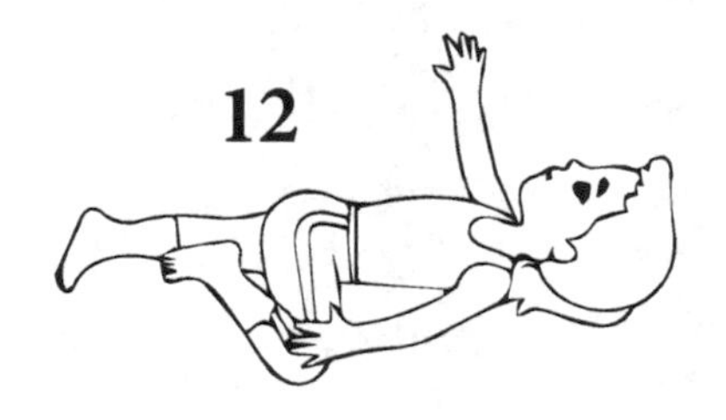

12. Seahorse is made by rotating the lower body at the hips and grabbing the right leg with the left hand. This move is one that truly works on motor planning and stretches the core musculature. Be sure to complete this pose on both sides to maintain blood flow and balance.

13. Star, windmill, or monkey is wonderful for lateral flexion and movement in the frontal plane. The child can choose to look up at his hand or down to his foot. Alternatives including holding the position while visually tracking. This is a huge challenge as the head is not in midline.

38. CRASH PAD

Crash pads are amazing in all settings and can be purchased or made of various soft materials. Many clinics choose to fill duvet covers with dense foam and can even get foam at deep discounts when purchased in bulk. Large beanbag chairs are also amazing crash pads. We stack Yogibo cushions and other soft, pillow-like items together and on top of slides and as a support for swings. Crash pads are ideal for a child who is having regulation difficulties, as he may feel comfortable crashing his body into a safe spot.

Jump on a trampoline and fall into a crash pad! Bounce on your peanut ball and crash into the beanbags. Swing while seated and jump into a crash mat! The possibilities are endless. Here are some of my favorite activities with crash mats:

- Use as part of an obstacle course to climb over, roll, or tumble on.
- Make snow angels; imitate animal movements while on the pad.

- Drag the mat as heavy work/proprioceptive input.
- Throw weighted/medicine balls into it for regulation and to help control escalating behavior. It's a great substitution for hitting others.
- Use the crash pad as a mat to prevent and even encourage falls!
- Lie on pad while completing functional tasks.

Raina Koterba
Limitless Performance and Therapy, Cedar Grove, NJ
www.limitlessnj.com

39. INFLATABLE DOLPHIN

Activity Theme: Dolphin Olympics! (Obstacle course challenge)

SETUP: Apparatus can be used on its own or within an obstacle course.

DESCRIPTION: Child can try to hold a tall kneel as long as possible. Crawl over the apparatus as part of an obstacle course. Have the child climb up on it and see how long he can hold different poses that an Olympic athlete might perform. Next, have him try to bend and pick up the pretend gold, silver, and bronze medals from the dolphin and stand to place them onto his neck.

Fun and Function
www.funandfunction.com

THERAPEUTIC BENEFITS: Improves core stability and upper-body strengthening, body awareness, sequencing, motor planning, vestibular and proprioceptive input, LE strengthening, and work in all planes.

ADAPT/GRADE: Inflate mattress less/more.

40. SCOOTER BOARD

A scooter board is an invaluable tool in every setting. The best part is that no suspension equipment is required, yet the vestibular and proprioceptive systems truly get a workout when a child plays with a scooter board. Flexion/extension, lateral flexion bilaterally, and trunk rotation can all be achieved by fun games on the scooter.

Affix a bungee cord across the clinic parallel to the child and use as the child pulls himself along on the scooter as he pretends to hang clothes or complete activities with clothespins or clips, or use perpendicular to the child to push and pull off of (rocket blastoffs).

Fun and Function
www.funandfunction.com

Activity Theme
Scooter Board Bungee Challenge

SETUP: Bungee cord across the clinic, perpendicular to the child. Arrange scooter board and bowling pins in a typical bowling fashion.

DESCRIPTION: Lie on the swing in supine position and use the bungee cord to self-propel backward into the bowling pins. Try to get a strike!

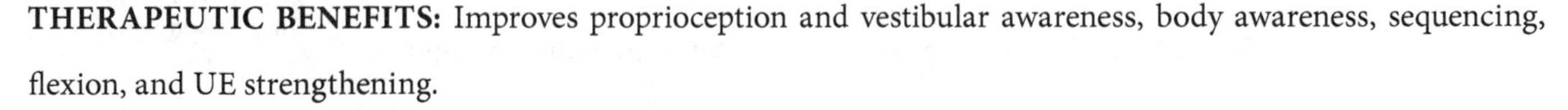

THERAPEUTIC BENEFITS: Improves proprioception and vestibular awareness, body awareness, sequencing, flexion, and UE strengthening.

ADAPT/GRADE: Adapt the scooter board bungee bowling challenge by using a wedge to promote neck and trunk flexion.

Here are some ideas:

- Use Squigz (or make one from plungers) to row your boat and move from side to side.
- While in supine position, use the feet to push a large therapy ball.
- Prone/supine/short kneel scooter board with bungee rope.
- Supine/prone kick offs from ball or wall.
- Kickoff to crash towers off blocks and through Hula-Hoops.
- Use a scooter ramp and crash into pad at the bottom.
- Use a rope to climb in supine position up the scooter ramp.
- In prone position, blow a whistle to pretend the child is a boat while you push his feet.
- In prone position, the child pulls on a Hula-Hoop held by a therapist.
- Follow a taped path in different directions.

- Pull child as he holds onto a rope.
- While seated, pretend the child is a crab and play soccer using feet only.
- Complete an obstacle course in all positions!

41. BALANCE BOARD

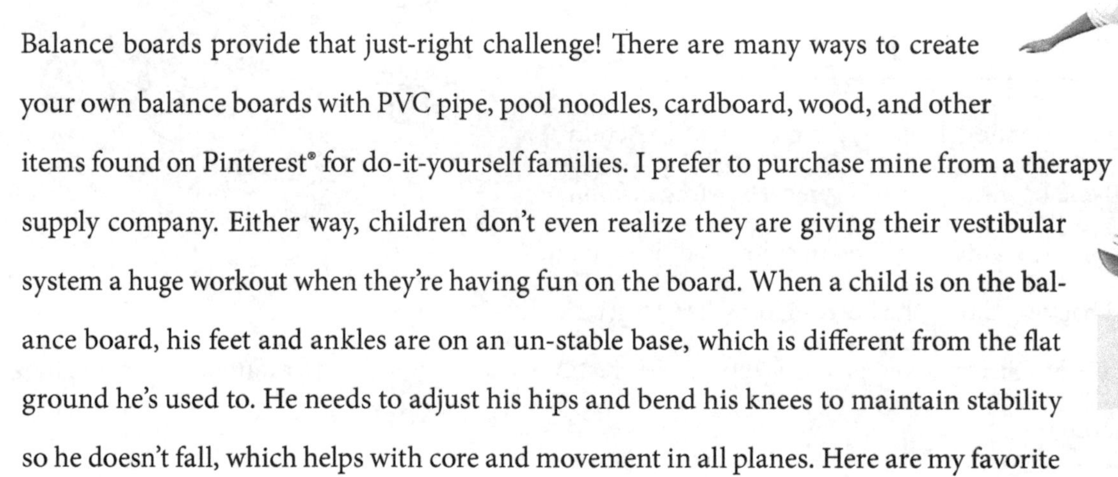

Southpaw Enterprises
www.southpaw.com

Balance boards provide that just-right challenge! There are many ways to create your own balance boards with PVC pipe, pool noodles, cardboard, wood, and other items found on Pinterest® for do-it-yourself families. I prefer to purchase mine from a therapy supply company. Either way, children don't even realize they are giving their vestibular system a huge workout when they're having fun on the board. When a child is on the balance board, his feet and ankles are on an un-stable base, which is different from the flat ground he's used to. He needs to adjust his hips and bend his knees to maintain stability so he doesn't fall, which helps with core and movement in all planes. Here are my favorite activities on a balance board:

- Toss/catch a ball back and forth. To grade the activity down, try a Velcro® ball.
- Ask children to bend down to pick up beanbags, stuffed animals, or balls. Toss them into a Hula-Hoop basketball hoop across the room (I find Hula-Hoops to be another extremely beneficial therapy tool).
- Complete animal moves and imitate how animals would act upon command.
- Do song dances such as "The Hokey Pokey," "Elephant Walk," and "Head, Shoulders, Knees, and Toes."
- Toss rings onto a T-ball stand. To make task easier, move the stand closer to the child.
- Play light saber games with each other.
- Stand on one foot at a time.
- Bend to the ground to pick up items.
- Try different yoga poses.
- For a real challenge, have the child close her eyes! Make a noise and ask the child to turn her body toward where she thinks the sound is coming from.

42. REFERENCES

Anderson-Hanley C, Tureck K, Schneiderman RL. Autism and exergaming: effects on repetitive behaviors and cognition. *Psychol Res Behav Manag.* 2011;4:129–137. Free Article.

Barnhart R, et al. Developmental Coordination Disorder. *Journal of the American Physical Therapy Association.* 2003; 83:722-731.

Benson, TA, Teasdale, A, Gentil, JLD, Gravitational Insecurity in Children with Sensory Integration and Processing Problems. *American Journal of Occupational Therapy 2016*;70(4_Supplement_1):7011500020p1. doi: 10.5014/ajot.2016.70S1-PO2007.

Baranek, GT Efficacy of Sensory and Motor Interventions of Children with Autism. *J Autism Dev Disord* (2002) 32: 397. doi:10.1023/A:1020541906063

Bhat AN, Landa RJ, Galloway JC. Current perspectives on motor functioning in infants, children, and adults with autism spectrum disorders. *Phys Ther. 2011*;91(7):1116–1129. Free Article.

Cartwright, JHE, Piro, O, & Tuval, I (2009). Fluid dynamics in developmental biology: moving fluids that shape ontogeny. *HFSP Journal*, 3(2), 77–93. http://doi.org/10.2976/1.

Chiba, R, Ogawa, H, Takakusaki, K, Asama, H, Ota, J. Muscle activities changing model by difference in sensory inputs on human posture control *Adv. Intell. Syst. Comput.*, 194 (2013), pp. 479–491

Chu, VWT, Bodison, S, Deficits in Proprioception Measured in Children with Somatodyspraxia. *American Journal of Occupational Therapy*, August 2016, Vol. 70, 7011500062p1. doi:10.5014/ajot.2016.70S1-PO5120

Doumas, M, McKenna, R, Murphy, BJ. *Autism Dev Disord (2016).* 46: 853. doi:10.1007/s10803-015-2621-4

Downey R, Rapport MJ. Motor activity in children with autism: a review of current literature. *Pediatric Phys Ther. 2012*;24(1):2–20. Article Summary in PubMed.

Dunn, RP, Levinthal, DJ, Strick, PL. Motor, cognitive, and affective areas of the cerebral cortex influence the adrenal medulla. *Biological Sciences—Neuroscience. PNAS 2016* 113 (35) 9922-9927; published ahead of print August 15, 2016, doi:10.1073/pnas.1605044113

Dziuk M, Gidley Larson JC, Apostu A, Mahone EM, Denckla MB, Mostofsky SH. Dyspraxia in autism: association with motor, social, and communicative deficits. *Dev Med Child Neurol.* 2007;49(10):734–739. Free Article.

Fong S, Ng S, Yiu B. Slowed muscle force production and sensory organization deficits contribute to altered postural control strategies in children with developmental coordination disorder. 2013; 34: 3040-3048.

Fragala-Pinkham MA, Haley SM, O'Neil ME. Group swimming and aquatic exercise programme for children with autism spectrum disorders: a pilot study. *Dev Neurorehabil. 2011*;14(4):230–241. Article Summary in *PubMed.*

Glumac, L, Pallai, B, Tartick, K, Savard, L, Baker, M, Greeley, K, Millkavich, L. Causes and Identification: Causes of Developmental Coordination Disorder. CanChild. McMaster University. https://canchild.ca/en/diagnoses/developmental-coordination-disorder/causes-identification

Grabowski, K. "The Role of the Speech Language Pathologist in the Neonatal Intensive Care Unit" (2013). Research Papers. Paper 359. http://opensiuc.lib.siu.edu/gs_rp/359

Gregory-Flock, JL, Yerxa, EJ. (1984). Standardization of the Prone Extension Postural Test on Children Ages 4 Through 8. *The American Journal of Occupational Therapy*, 38, 187-194. doi:10.5014/ajot.38.3.187

Jamon, M. "The Development of Vestibular System and Related Functions in Mammals: Impact of Gravity." Frontiers in Integrative *Neuroscience 8* (2014): 11. PMC. Web. 27 Mar. 2017.

Jelsma D, et al. Short-term learning of dynamic balance control in children with probable Developmental Coordination Disorder. *Research in Developmental Disabilities.* 2015; 38: 213-222.

Karim, H, Fuhrman, SI, Sparto, P, Furman, J, Huppert, T. Functional brain imaging of multi-sensory vestibular processing during computerized dynamic posturography using near-infrared spectroscopy *Neuroimage*, 74 (2013), pp. 318–325

Lefkof, MB. Trunk Flexion In Healthy Children Ages 3 to 7 Years. *Physical Therapy.* Volume 66. No.1, January 1986: 39-44

McLean, WJ, Dalton, T, McLean, RAE, Edge, ASB, Distinct capacity for differentiation to inner ear cell types by progenitor cells of the cochlea and vestibular organs. *Development.* 2016. 143: 4381-4393; doe: 10.1242/dev.139840

Speedtsberg, Merete B, SB, Christensen, K., Kjøller, A, Jesper B, Jensen, BR, Curtis, DJ. Impaired postural control in children with developmental coordination disorder is related to less efficient central as well as peripheral control, *Gait & Posture*, Volume 51, January 2017, Pages 1-6, ISSN 0966-6362, http://doi.org/10.1016/j.gaitpost.2016.09.019. (http://www.sciencedirect.com/science/article/pii/S0966636216305811)

National Autism Center. National standards project: findings and conclusions/addressing the needs for evidence-based practice guidelines for autism spectrum disorders. National Autism Center website. Accessed August 6, 2014.

Nobile M, Perego P, Piccinini L, et al. Further evidence of complex motor dysfunction in drug naive children with autism using automatic motion analysis of gait. *Autism.* 2011; 15(3):263–283. Article Summary in *PubMed.*

Rinehart, N, McGinley, J. Is motor dysfunction core to autism spectrum disorder? *Dev Med Child Neurol. 2010*; 52(8):697. Free Article.

Robledo, J, Donnellan, AM, Strandt-Conroy, K. An Exploration of Sensory and Movement Differences from the Pespective of Invididuals with Autism, *Frontiers in Integrative Neuroscience*, 16 November, 2012.

Roley, SS, Maillouw, Z, Parham, LD, Schaaf, RC, Lane, CJ, Cermak, S. Sensory Integration and Praxis Patterns in Children with Autism. *American Journal of Occupational Therapy*, December 2014, Vol. 69, 6901220010p1-6901220010p8. doi:10.5014/ajot.2015.012476

Ryosuke Chiba, Kaoru Takakusaki, Jun Ota, Arito Yozu, Nobuhiko Haga, Human upright posture control models based on multisensory inputs; in fast and slow dynamics, *Neuroscience Research*, Volume 104, March 2016, Pages 96-104, ISSN 0168-0102, http://doi.org/10.1016/j.neures.2015.12.002.

(http://www.sciencedirect.com/science/article/pii/S0168010215002928)

Keywords: Posture control; Multisensory integration; Long-term alteration; Body representation in brain; Balance

Sellers, JE. Relationship Between Antigravity Control and Postural Control in Young Children. *Physical Therapy.* 1988;486-490.

Sensory Processing Disorder Foundation http://www.spdfoundation.net/about-sensory-processing-disorder/redsflags/

Sowa, M, Meulenbroek, R. Effects of physical exercise on autism spectrum disorders: a meta-analysis. *Res Autism Spectr Disord.* 2012;6:46–57. Free Abstract here.

Srinivasan SM, Pescatello LS, Bhat AN. Current perspectives on physical activity and exercise recommendations for children and adolescents with autism spectrum disorders. *Phys Ther.* 2014;94(6):875–889. Article Summary in *PubMed.*

Westcott, SL1, Lowes, LP, Richardson, PK. Evaluation of postural stability in children: current theories and assessment tools. *Physical Therapy.* 1997. Jun;77(6):629-45

SENSORIMOTOR INTERVENTIONS ASSESSMENT

Posture	Rating Scale			
	Normal	Mild asymmetry/ roundness	Moderate asymmetry/ roundness	Severe asymmetry/ roundness
Shoulder symmetry				
Shoulder roundness				
Slouching during fine motor tasks				
Spinal curvature *(circle one)*	Normal	Scoliosis left	Scoliosis right	Notes:
	Note position		Note abnormalities	
Position while seated on floor				
Position while seated in chair				

Position	Rating Scale			
	Able to move into position	Time position sustained	Smoothness of movement	Notes:
Supine Flexion				
Prone Extension				
Stand on right foot				
Stand on left foot				
Hopping on one foot				
	No difficulty	Mild difficulty	Moderate diff.	Severe or unable
Walking straight line pigeon (toes in)				
Walking straight line duck (toes out)				
Sit-ups				
Push-ups (note type)				
Hop over line Feet together				
Jumping Jacks				
Skipping				
Rolling				
Postural changes on un-even surfaces				
Crawl in quadruped position				

DIFFICULTIES NOTED MAY INCLUDE:

- Complaints of nausea, dizzy, vertigo
- Falling
- Displacing the supporting foot
- Compensatory trunk, mouth, shoulder, or other movement
- Avoidance or refusal
- Connection between upper and lower halves of body
- Difficulty or unable to cross body midline
- Movement of the body in segments (when rolling)
- Positions preferred for stability both in chair and on floor

MAKE NOTE OF:

- Adaptive equipment or specialized seating adaptations such as Theraband for proprioceptive input
- Child's balance is: normal, clumsy, emerging skills, precarious
- Presence of retained reflexes such as ATNR and moro
- Presence of abnormal or extraneous movements of body

ORAL-MOTOR CONCERNS

- Note chewing performance: Is child using lateral and rotary chew, or immature chewing pattern?
- Note whether child is stuffing and/or pocketing of food
- Is there choking or coughing during and after eating?
- Are there extra mouth or jaw movements when concentrating?
- Is child a messy eater or has decreased awareness of food/mess on face?

Activity	Rating Scale			
	Normal	Deficits noted	Child complaints	Notes:
Tracking *(perform both convergence and divergence)*				
Saccades				
Pursuits				
Convergence				
Gaze stabilization				
Fix gaze and turn body + head				
Fix gaze + head turn body				

VISION ASSESSMENT TRACKING (AROM) INSTRUCTIONS

- Hold target 16 inches from child and instruct to keep head still while moving eyes only.
- OT moves target toward tip of child's nose. Stop when student reports seeing two of the object or when touching nose.
- Note any dissociative head and eye movements.
- Make sure to track in all directions: horizontal, vertical, diagonal, circular (clockwise and counter-clockwise).
- Note any deviation of either eye.
- Convergence = toward the nose.
- Divergence = away from the nose.
- Nystagmus = small, rhythmic movement of eyes *Neurology referral*.

WHY SACCADES AND PURSUITS?

- Saccades are used every day by all of us. When we read or scan a picture, we look from point to point to make sense of what we are looking at. When reading, we move our eyes from letter to letter.
- Saccades are quick movements with short duration.
- When driving, we use saccades to look from a street sign to our speedometer. Each is fixed in position.
- A pursuit is the ability of our eyes to follow moving targets.
- Children watch the ball as it's thrown in the game. When driving, we look at moving cars and then back to the road as we move along.

VISION ASSESSMENT SACCADES INSTRUCTIONS

- Goal is to focus on a specific point (shifting between two points) as quickly as possible.
- This is a sudden change of vision from point to point.
- OT sits knee to knee or stands (2–3 feet from child's eyes).
- Use two different colored markers or items that the child can recognize and look at when named.
- Hold items in vertical plane at least one foot from each other and call out each item. For instance, if using two markers: pink, yellow, pink, yellow. If using thumb and finger: thumb, finger, thumb, finger.
- Repeat in horizontal plane.
- Note whether or not both eyes move at the same time.
- Note any dissociative head and eye movements.
- Is eye movement accurate?
- Can child find the target?

VISION ASSESSMENT PURSUITS INSTRUCTIONS

- Goal is to watch moving targets.
- OT sits knee to knee or stands (2–3 feet from child's eyes).
- Use two different colored markers or items that the child can recognize and look at when named.
- Slowly move items in all planes at least a foot from each other and call out each item. For instance, if using two markers: pink, yellow, pink, yellow.

- Note whether both eyes move at the same time.
- Note any dissociative head, body, and eye movements.
- Is eye movement accurate?
- Can child find the targets?

GAZE STABILIZATION INSTRUCTIONS

- Look at an item such as a pencil or index card placed at eye-level and at least two feet from the child.
- Keep looking at the item and move head at a 45-degree angle to the right and then to the left.
- Note whether or not both eyes move at the same time.
- Note any dissociative head, body, and eye movements.
- Is eye movement accurate?
- Can child keep focus on the target?

VISION CONCERNS

- Nystagmus
- Crossing of eyes
- Complaints of double vision, headaches, watery eyes, difficulty reading
- Note preference for light vs. dark
- Note glasses vs. contacts
- Sensitivity to fluorescent lighting
- Prefers certain colors of paper

ASSESSMENT REFERENCES

Antonucci MM, Osthus T and Esposito SE (2016). Treatment of attention deficit disorder using vestibular and gaze therapy. Front. Neurol. Conference Abstract: *International Symposium on Clinical Neuroscience: Clinical Neuroscience for Optimization of Human Function*. doi: 10.3389/conf.fneur.2016.59.00008

Braswell, J., Rine, R. M., "Preliminary Evidence of Improved Gaze Stability Following Exercise in Two Children with Vestibular Hypofunction." *International Journal of Pediatric Otorhinolaryngology* 70 (2006): 70.11. Web.19 Apr. 2017. • Children's Hospital of California: http://www.choc.org/video/concussion-homeexercise-vestibular-ocular-gaze-stabilization/

Rajendran, Venkadesan, and Finita Glory Roy. "An Overview of Motor Skill Performance and Balance in Hearing Impaired Children." *Italian Journal of Pediatrics* 37 (2011): 33. PMC. Web. 19 Apr. 2017.

ABOUT THE AUTHOR

Pediatric occupational therapist Cara Koscinski, MOT, OTR/L, is the author of *The Parent's Guide to Occupational Therapy for Autism and Special Needs*, *The Special Needs SCHOOL Survival Guide*, and *The Weighted Blanket Guide—Everything You Need to Know About Weighted Blankets and Deep Pressure for Autism, Chronic Pain, and Other Conditions.* She has successfully founded two pediatric therapy clinics and has produced CDs for children with autism and auditory sensitivity. As The Pocket Occupational Therapist, Cara provides OT consultations, trainings, CEUs, and seminars on autism, behavior, sensory, and movement. Ms. Koscinski is on the advisory board for *Autism Asperger's Digest* and *Asperkids.* Cara's own two children have autism, and she has received extensive training in behavior, sensory processing, and movement integration. Cara is a certified children's YOGA instructor. Articles and courses by Cara have been featured in many publications, including *Parents Magazine*, *Advance for Occupational Therapy*, *Autism Asperger's Digest*, *Of Course Learning*, and *Autism File.* She is a continuing education provider for many companies in the US and the UK.

Yoga photos by

For additional information, photos, links to helpful downloads, evaluation videos in Cara's clinic, and more: Please visit the website exclusively available for those who purchase this book:

http://www.pocketot.com/sensorimotorinterventions

Password: BuildingBetterBrainsCourse

Facebook: https://www.facebook.com/PocketOT

Twitter: @PocketOT

Also by the Author

The Special Needs SCHOOL Survival Guide is THE handbook that will answer your questions about school accommodations, handwriting, autism, SPD (Sensory Processing Disorder) in the classroom, learning disabilities, ADHD, IEPs, behavior, dysgraphia, and more. It contains easy-to-follow school activities. The Q&A format makes the book easy to read. This book will prove to be a resource you will use frequently as your student with special needs progresses through school.

Printed in the USA
CPSIA information can be obtained
at www.ICGtesting.com
JSHW051459300923
49249JS00001B/1